ASSESSING HEALTH NEED USING THE LIFE CYCLE FRAMEWORK

Chrissie Pickin and
Selwyn St Leger

Open University Press
Buckingham • *Philadelphia*

Open University Press
Celtic Court
22 Ballmoor
Buckingham
MK18 1XW

and
1900 Frost Road, Suite 101
Bristol, PA 19007, USA

First Published 1993

A catalogue record of this book is available from the
British Library

Library of Congress Cataloging-in-Publication Data

Pickin, Chrissie, 1959–
    Assessing health need using the life cycle framework/Chrissie
Pickin and Selwyn St Leger.
        p. cm.
    Includes bibliographical references.
    ISBN 0–335–15742–4 (pb).—ISBN 0–335–15743–2 (hb)
    1. Health status indicators—Great Britain. 2. Life cycle, Human.
3. Health status indicators. I. St Leger, A. S. (Antony Selwyn),
1948– . II. Title.
    [DNLM: 1. Health Services—organization & administration.
2. Health Services Needs and Demand. WA 525 P597a]
RA407.5.G7P53 1992
362.1'068—dc20
DNLM/DLC
for Library of Congress   92–18760
                                                                      CIP

Typeset by Graphicraft Typesetters Ltd, Hong Kong
Printed in Great Britain by Biddles Ltd, Guildford and Kings Lynn

CONTENTS

PREFACE

This book is addressed to those who seek to assess the health needs of populations in a systematic manner. Matching resources for health, in particular services, to needs is the core task of health services policy making and planning. Policy making and planning encompass the skills of diverse people. These range from professional managers through public health physicians, whose 'patients' are populations rather than individuals, to those health professionals and others who daily try to meet the needs of the particular clients or patients with whom they are in contact. Each has much to contribute: managers and public health physicians from their broad perspective of aggregate need and of the requirement to plan services within fixed resources; clinicians, nurses, health care professionals and others through their intimate knowledge of what their disciplines have to offer and through their direct contact with those whom they serve.

Within the United Kingdom, health needs assessment has come to the fore as a consequence of the NHS and Community Care Act 1990. This provides a structure within which the health needs of defined populations have to be assessed and packages of services planned and purchased (on behalf of the community) to meet, as far as feasible, those needs. Of course the UK is not unique in this. All countries plan at least some health-related services on behalf of their populations. The degree to which this is controlled by the state varies. However, in both socialized and insurance-based health schemes some kind of systematic needs assessment is desirable. Needs assessment is a *rational basis* for the subsequent disbursement of resources among needs groups.

Needs assessment is wide-ranging and we explore some of its broader ramifications in Chapters 2 and 15. However, the focus of this book is very precise. It is concerned with the structuring of one's thinking about the assessment of health need and with the organization of information pertaining to health need. It proposes an intellectual framework within which to embed some key elements of health needs assessment. This structure, the *life cycle framework*, brings together biological, social, environmental and cultural influences on health need in a manner which aids doing health needs assessment in a coherent way. The book, however, is *not* a manual of techniques for making particular assessments of health status or health need. These techniques abound and the literature on them is vast, but what is lacking, and *what we addre*ss, is a clarity of context within which to employ them.

The ideas presented in this book are not fanciful theory: they are being employed successfully in the North West of England and elsewhere. We stumbled upon the life cycle framework when we were commissioned by the North Western Regional Health Authority to produce an 'information tool-box' to assist Family Health Service Authority (FHSA) managers to undertake health needs assessment. It rapidly became clear to us that the traditional 'shopping list' approach to assembling information sources does not convey clarity of purpose. The essentially simple idea of the life cycle framework enabled us to present health needs and their determinants in a manner which dictates information requirements. The *information tool-box*, which was published on a small scale by the regional health authority, was warmly received by its intended readership. To our surprise it was also welcomed and found useful by many colleagues in public health medicine whom we had assumed would not require such an aid, as they already possess considerable knowledge and skills pertaining to needs assessment. The life cycle framework is also being used in training courses for executive and non-executive members of FHSAs and district health authorities. Most unexpected of all was the discovery that our life cycle framework is being used as a basis for teaching public health to medical undergraduates at the University of Liverpool; the sections of the course are founded on each of our life cycle stages.

This book is an expansion of the publication mentioned above. It is aimed at a wide readership: all those who seek a coherent view of health needs assessment in the context of populations. These include policy makers, service managers, planners, diverse doctors (especially fund holding general practitioners), nurses (especially health visitors), practitioners and trainees in public health, members of professions (e.g. social workers) who collaborate with health professionals, and undergraduates in medicine and nursing.

In order to accommodate the varying backgrounds of our readership we have made no assumptions about their prior knowledge of epidemiological concepts and the interpretation of quantitative health data. Furthermore, we do not assume familiarity with the sociological approaches to collecting information on health needs. Chapters 3 and 4 provide an elementary and sufficient introduction to these to allow full understanding of the life cycle framework. The theoretical underpinnings and use of the framework are introduced in Chapter 5. Chapters 6 to 14 detail each of our life cycle stages.

We do not anticipate, nor necessarily recommend, that Chapters 6 to 14 be read in sequence, although a quick skim through them will assist the reader to understand the nature and structure of the information presented. Each of these chapters is self-contained and should be viewed as a resource to be tapped when required. In consequence there is some repetition of material about data sources etc. We consider this preferable to sending the reader hither and thither through extensive cross-referencing.

It should be noted that we have been selective in our referencing of source materials. In the chapters surrounding those pertaining to the life cycle stages we have referenced where appropriate. However, in Chapters 6 to 14 we have, for clarity of presentation, not referenced the many statements, e.g. that perinatal mortality rates are statistically associated with occupational social class, which we consider to belong to a common currency of accepted knowledge in public health. The sources of that knowledge are cited in books in our further reading list, e.g. the Black Report and other standard texts in the relevant fields. Our prime aim has been to cover a wide area and not to lose sight of the wood for the trees.

ACKNOWLEDGEMENTS

The ideas presented in this book arose when we were commissioned by the North Western Regional Health Authority to prepare an information tool-box to assist Family Health Services Authority managers to undertake health needs assessment. We are indebted to many colleagues in the health service and the University of Manchester who helped us refine these ideas and put them into practice. We are particularly grateful to Dr S. D. Horsley (Regional Medical Officer) and Dr J. P. Walsworth-Bell (Regional Consultant in Public Health Medicine) for support and encouragement and for their permission, on behalf of the regional health authority, to use our material from the original information tool-box in this book. Also, we thank Ms Ailsa Morrant from public dental health for her contribution to the work.

A work of this kind draws upon knowledge from diverse fields. In particular, our experience as public health physicians has given us insight into the valuable contribution of medical sociology. However, we did not regard ourselves as competent to introduce this field to our readers. Thus, we are greatly indebted to Jennie Popay and Dr Gareth Williams for writing Chapter 4. Jennie Popay is Director of the Public Health Research and Resource Centre for the Bolton, Salford, Trafford and Wigan Health Authorities, and based in the Salford Royal Hospital,

Salford. Gareth Williams is Senior Research Fellow in the Sociology of Health and Illness at the Centre for Health Studies, University College Salford, and the Department of Sociology, the University of Salford.

We thank Professor H. Schnieden and Dr J. P. Walsworth Bell for permission to reproduce a table and a slightly modified version of an appendix on information sources from the book (of which A. S. St Leger was a co-author) entitled *Evaluating Health Services' Effectiveness* (Open University Press 1992).

We are grateful to Mr A. Mercer and Dr N. Unwin for permission to reproduce their schema for purchasing in Figure 15.1.

Our grateful thanks go to friends and colleagues who supported us through the process of writing, in particular Jan Williams.

ABBREVIATIONS

AIDS	acquired immune-deficiency syndrome
DHA	district health authority
DoH	Department of Health (of the UK government)
ED	enumeration district
FHSA	family health services authority
GDP	general dental practitioner
GP	general (medical) practitioner
HAA	hospital activity analysis
HIV	human immune-deficiency virus
KARS	Körner Aggregated Returns System
KES	Körner Episode System
MMR	measles, mumps and rubella vaccine
NHS	National Health Service
NHSME	National Health Service Management Executive
NSPCC	National Society for the Prevention of Cruelty to Children
OPCS	Office of Population, Censuses and Surveys
PI	performance indicator
PNMR	perinatal mortality rate
RHA	regional health authority
SIDS	sudden infant death syndrome

SMR   standardized mortality ratio
STD   sexually transmitted disease
WHO   World Health Organization

Note: some of these abbreviations and many other terms employed in this work are explained in the Glossary.

1 THE NEW NHS – OPPORTUNITIES AND CHALLENGES

It is widely recognised that the provision of health services should be informed by an assessment of health needs in the Region or District concerned, combined with evaluation of the extent to which services provided successfully tackle those needs.

Thus stated the Department of Health circular (E(88)64) in response to the Acheson report, 'Public Health in England'.[1] After 40 years of the National Health Service there had begun a debate about health and health need rather than health services. As Popper has suggested,[2] in exploring any new field of interest it is probably less useful to define terms than to define the problems that the new area is seeking to address. Therefore, rather than looking at definitions of health, need and assessment, we will examine the problems with health service planning in the late 1980s that the introduction of health needs assessment sought to address. It should then become clear what health needs assessment should be.

In 1988/9 approximately £26 billion was spent on the health service[3] yet we had very little idea of just what benefit this was achieving for the general population. The problem seemed to be that health service planning was supply-led, and focused on services and in particular hospital care. In many cases the local health service was felt to be inappropriate to the needs of the local population. How had this situation arisen?

THE PRE-REFORMATION NHS

In 1989, despite occasional tinkering and re-structuring, the essential character of the NHS had remained unchanged from its inception in 1948. Funds were distributed from the centre through various tiers of management down to units (e.g. hospitals) and thence to support the activities of diverse clinical (and community) specialisms. Latterly, the tiers of management have been the NHS Management Board, regional health authorities (14 in England), district health authorities and unit management, each of the lower tiers being accountable to a higher one. District health authorities were responsible for planning services for their resident populations and also for managing units sited within their boundaries. Generally, units had catchment populations extending beyond the geographical bounds of their corresponding health authority resident populations; conversely, a proportion of any resident population would have their needs met by services provided by a different health authority. The funding allocated to a district was based on the size of the resident population and crudely weighted for need; this was then adjusted to account for net cross-boundary flows.

It was difficult for district health authorities to reconcile their managerial responsibility for units with their other remit to plan services for their resident populations. The practical problems of financing and managing hospitals tended to dominate. Moreover, it is hard to plan services for a geographically defined population once boundary flows and catchment populations come into the equation. The major exception to this was community services (child immunization and vaccination, health visiting etc.), which were planned and distributed on a resident population basis.

Another problem was that primary care services were financially, managerially and, to a large extent, functionally divorced from secondary care and community services. Given that general practitioners are the acknowledged gate-keepers to secondary care and that there should be a great deal in common between primary care and community services, this separation was particularly irksome.

A major problem with the pre-reformation NHS was that its planning, information and managerial procedures allowed few ways of coping with resource constraints. Throughout most of the history of the NHS, funding grew in real terms (i.e. above inflation). Thus, it appeared that demands for more, bigger and better services consequent upon medical innovation, public expectations and demographic drift could be coped with. To an extent this was true but some of the cost of extra demand was met by allowing already poor hospital stock to deteriorate further. Real growth and neglect of capital stock enabled politicians and managers to stave off having to face up to the fact that there must be some finite amount society is willing to spend on health, and that living within a fixed budget entails making difficult choices.

The imposition of strict cash limits on health spending in the 1980s brought these problems to prominence. Despite improvements in efficiency brought about by the introduction of modern managerial practices[4] the shortfall of funds became apparent. Demand exceeding supply leads, in a free health service, to rationing. The growing hospital waiting lists became a political issue to which the government responded by tweaking the tail of NHS management and demanding quick fixes. Potential and actual overspends of budgets led to crisis rationing: the dramatic closure of beds or wards. The moral is that if explicit selection among choices is not made while there is leeway for considered thought then drastic, usually non-optimum, solutions are forced upon one later.[5]

It is interesting to note that hospital consultants are the individuals with most influence on how NHS resources are disbursed. Rarely was management sufficiently confident (or possibly competent) to seek justification of their stewardship. Moreover, too often service developments with considerable revenue implications were allowed to creep along in an unplanned manner as consultants altered the nature and content of their practices.[6] However, it must be mentioned that no one was in a position to give them a detailed breakdown of the resources they used. The need to give consultants this information was the rationale behind the introduction of Resource Management[7] into the NHS in 1987.

THE REFORMS

Cost control is one of the central issues for socialized and insurance-based health services. It appears to be the major motivation for the reforms contained in the NHS and Community Care Act 1990, which came into force in April 1991. The key elements of interest here are:

- separation of the responsibility of commissioning health services ('purchasers') from the responsibility of managing services ('providers');
- creation of an internal NHS market whereby providers (e.g. hospitals) compete to sell services to purchasers;
- reorganization of the financing and management of primary care services (e.g. Family Health Service Authorities replacing Family Practitioner Committees);
- giving certain general practitioners the option to hold a budget for the purchase of a variety of services for their patients.

Purchasers commission services for the resident populations of district health authorities. They now have a budget based mainly on the size and age structure of their resident populations; it is crudely weighted to allow for the differing needs of various populations. The budget no longer takes account of the costs, workload or flow of patients to provider units that happen to be located within the authority's boundaries.

At present many district health authorities have both purchaser and provider responsibilities; they are supposed to maintain a 'Chinese wall' between them. The ultimate intent is that all provider units will become independently managed NHS trusts accountable directly to the Secretary of State for Health. The pace at which this will happen is determined by the financial viability of existing units.

FHSAs are beginning to merge with the purchasing arms of DHAs to form common purchasing teams for all primary, community and secondary care services. This has enormous advantages in encouraging the integration between primary and secondary care as well as concentrating scarce skills and producing economy of scale. The question is whether these changes will allow the development of a health service which can respond to local needs while maintaining the financial and political control required by any central government.

The deliberations of the NHS review *Working for Patients*,[8] which led to the NHS and Community Care Act, were more wide-ranging than many had expected and attempted to address many of the fundamental problems of a centralized health service by proposing this purchaser–provider split. Although using a market terminology, this is essentially a split between strategic and operational management. The paper further emphasized the purchasing or commissioning role of health authorities as involving assessment of the health needs of the local population and appraisal of service options to meet those needs.

Thus the scene was set for a radical change in the way the NHS could be run. Could strategic planning be introduced to address both short- and long-term health needs? Could planning in the NHS begin to look at where we wanted to be in the future rather than serving 'the dominant paradigms and interests of what is rather than what could be'?[9] The tools to begin this process were the purchaser–provider split and assessment of health need.

REFERENCES

1 The Report of the Committee of Inquiry into Public Health Function (1988) *Public Health in England* (Acheson Report). London: HMSO.
2 Popper, K. (1976) *Unended Quest – An Intellectual Biography*. London: Fontana/Collins, pp. 17–31.
3 Chartered Institute for Public Finance and Accountancy (1989) *Health Service Trends*, 2nd edn. London: CIPFA.
4 Department of Health and Social Security (1983) *National Health Service Management Enquiry* (Griffith Report). London: HMSO.
5 Heginbotham, C. (1992) Rationing. *British Medical Journal*, **304**, 496–9.

6 Schnieden, H. and Grimes, M. (1989) Audit and performance indicators: a case study in ophthalmology. *Journal of Mangement in Medicine*, **3**, 301–14.
7 British Medical Association (1989) *An Evaluation of the Six Experimental Sites by the Central Consultants and Specialists Committee of the British Medical Association*. London: Resource Management Initiative, BMA.
8 Department of Health (1989) *Working for Patients*. London: HMSO.
9 Small, N. (1989) *Politics and Planning in the National Health Service*. Milton Keynes: Open University Press.

2 / WHAT IS HEALTH NEEDS ASSESSMENT?

The important things about health needs assessment are, first, that it is a process not a task and, second, that it is of no benefit of itself; it is merely a tool to achieve a needs-led approach to planning and purchasing. It is not just the identification of health problems in a community (which is a health status profile or health needs identification). *Essentially, health needs assessment is the process of exploring the relationship between health problems in a community and the resources available to address those problems in order to achieve a desired outcome.*

Health problems, however, are more than medical problems and health resources are more than health care resources. Although the amount and type of health care is important, health is determined by much more than formal health care and therefore the resources available to address health problems are much more than health services.

In the three years since the NHS review was published (1989) there have been many other definitions of health needs assessment.[1-5] However, all essentially follow two approaches. The dominant model so far has been to start with the present health care services and then to assess how many and what sort of people are in need of them. The assessment can then be used to make marginal changes in the volume and quality of health services for which they are in contract. The second model starts with the population and then explores which services or policies would best lead to their needs being met.

The Department of Health definition[1] of 'the ability to benefit from health care' has encouraged many people to concentrate their attention on the first model. Yet this way of thinking is unlikely to address the problems with health service planning present before assessment of health need was introduced. Focusing on people, not services, allows more scope for change as it encourages a much broader view of health and health care. This approach is more consistent with the public health perspective. It is also more difficult to carry out and is more difficult to fit into an existing health service planning structure. It is our contention, however, that the existing health service planning structure is a barrier to the development of a needs-led service and that we must move to a new approach if we are to maximize the benefit of the introduction of the purchaser–provider split to the public health.

THE ELEMENTS OF HEALTH NEEDS ASSESSMENT

The elements of health needs assessment are three-fold (see Table 2.1).

Measurement of health status and identification of health problems

The World Health Organization defines health as 'A state of physical, mental and social well-being, and not only the absence of disease and disability.' To measure this is a very large and daunting task at the moment but we can get some way towards it, although the timescale may be longer than is often recognized.

To measure comprehensively the health status of a community will require the development of a very large database, bringing together an enormous amount of information from a wide range of sources. It will include epidemiological measures of mortality, disease incidence and prevalence as well as measures of perceived health. There is also a pressing need to develop positive health indicators. For instance, how is a community's social well-being to be measured? There is a need to develop measures of social support and community spirit. There are measures of the mental illness in a community but we need to develop measures of the mental *health* of individuals and populations.

Much of the routinely available information will not be particularly useful for the identification and measurement of health problems in a community. The difficulty with many of the summary statistics used as measures of health in a population is that they aggregate information by age and gender, e.g. the standardized mortality ratio and the standardized fertility rate. This type of information allows for comparisons

Table 2.1 The elements of the assessment of health need

Health status measurement	Ways of maximizing health gain	Measurement of health resources
Disease occurrence		
mortality	Health education/promotion	Individual
morbidity	Health promotion	Family
risk factors	Community development	Community
	Community participation	
Disease occurrence 'modifiers'		*Health service provision*
socio-economic factors	FHSA liaison in	Primary care services
environmental factors	commissioning services	
ethnic factors	Contracting process	Secondary care services
cultural factors		Tertiary care services
Perceived health status	Local authority liaison	*Local authority services*
	Voluntary sector liaison	*Voluntary sector services*
Positive health indicators		*'Modifiers' to service utilization*
		socio-economic factors
		environmental factors
		ethnic factors
		cultural factors
	Lobbying	*National/local policies affecting health*

between areas and populations but is insufficient for health needs assessment; for example, how does one relate a standardized mortality ratio (SMR) to service provision of any kind? The problems arise because age and gender are two of the main determinants of health status at both an individual and a population level.

SMRs can be a good proxy for overall health in a community (see the discussion in Chapter 3). However, they do not explain *why* one district has worse health than another and they cannot be used to relate differences in health experience to service provision or to other health resources in a community. Age and gender influence not only health but also the use of health services. Two populations with the same SMR but with different age and gender structures of their populations will have entirely different service requirements.

The assessment of health need includes the need for preventive services as well as providing for those who are already ill. This, together with the fact that we need to attempt to predict future health needs as well as to respond to present ones, means that we will also require measures of those factors which modify the health experience of a community, such as socio-economic influences, geographical location, environmental hazards and conditions, ethnic group membership and customs, and local cultural factors influencing health. The views of the local people themselves will be vital in this area. The skills required to investigate and measure these include epidemiology, sociology, anthropology and social research.

To ensure that the information collected is easily accessible will require information technology skills, including systems analysis, data linkage etc. Consequently there will have to be very close links between departments of public health, and district health authority and FHSA information departments. However, much of the information will remain textual, i.e. reports, research findings etc. There is a need to develop a much broader information service than that in the past – what the NHS management executive has called an 'intelligence service'.[6]

Assessment of health resources

Assessing the health needs of a community will involve an assessment of the resources currently available to that community that help them to promote and maintain health as well as to cure disease. Health resources include those within individuals, those within families and those within the community. The last include primary, secondary and tertiary care provided by the health services, the local authority and the voluntary sector, e.g. soup kitchens, counselling services, abortion services and hospice provision.

To measure what is available will require the collection of routine health service activity data, statistics from the primary care services and statistics from the local authority, community studies and talking to field-workers and to people from the local community. This information must also be presented and held in an accessible form, although not all will be computerized.

Maximization of health gain

The next step is to relate the measurement of health status with the measurement of health resources and attempt to highlight action required to maximize the health benefit or *health gain* to the community. Thinking about gain in health forces us to focus on health, not health services, and on health outcomes rather than service processes. One of the most important steps is to identify what we are trying to achieve in health terms. That is, we need to define our desired outcomes at this stage; for example, in the case of visually impaired older people are we trying to achieve the best vision possible, the best function possible or the best quality of life? For pregnant women are we trying to achieve a healthy baby or a healthy baby and a happy mother? Determining our aims in outcome terms encourages an exploration of the relationship between identified health problems and health resources in a meaningful way. Service effectiveness evaluation and medical audit can help us to determine realistic public health aims or outcomes but we must not restrict the definition of outcomes to that which we can currently measure. Determining what we are trying to achieve will show us where we need to develop or improve our outcome measures.

Potential health resource options must be appraised according to pre-determined criteria. It is important to realize at this stage that health needs assessment is not value-free. Our value base will affect the health needs assessment process. More effective decision making is likely to result from our health needs assessment if that value base is made explicit and is shared by the organization as a whole. Many people, both lay and professional, may be involved in this process. The value system adopted will direct health needs assessment, the appraisal of options to meet needs and the decisions taken as a result of these.

Does the organization value equity in health or a utilitarian approach of increasing health overall in a community? Is local access more important than value for money? Is supporting carers more important than ensuring that crisis care is available? Do we value what the professionals say about service acceptability more than what the public say? Do we value primary care above secondary and tertiary care? These are all difficult questions to answer but our actions as purchasers will to some extent have been determined by our implicit answers to them. By being made explicit they are open to challenge but this makes it more likely that a common value system can be developed.

With our value system having been determined, there are many ways of maximizing health gain. Each purchasing organization needs to clarify the criteria it will use to judge options for maximizing health gain based on its value system.

At the present time commissioning or purchasing of health care is restricted to health service provision and to predominantly secondary and tertiary care services. In the future the range of services purchased or commissioned by health authorities may widen. Until that time, however, it is clear that we should not restrict our activities to the commissioning or purchasing of health care services. In particular, contracting for secondary and tertiary care services is not the only way in which health gain can be maximized.

The commissioning of primary care services is a very important way of increasing the health resources in an area and thus collaboration with the FHSA is essential. Increasing health resources in areas such as family competence in childcare or supporting voluntary sector provision may be the best way of increasing health gain in a community. It is for this reason that this book concentrates on the development of service options in primary care. Many people when they think of the health service think only of secondary care services. When we begin to explore the health problems in a community then the pivotal role of primary care becomes highlighted. The recent changes in the management of primary care services have meant that there is now much greater room to influence the development of primary care to meet identified health problems in a community.

Exploring the health problems in a community will also highlight the importance of the many local authority departments as a resource for health, e.g. housing department, highways department, leisure and re-creation services as well as the more obvious candidates of social services and education.

It should be recognized that professional definitions of benefit may differ from lay definitions. A process is needed by which the local community's perspective can be included in the decision making regarding relative health benefit.

NEEDS-LED PLANNING AND PRIORITIZATION

An assessment of health need is not of benefit for its own sake. Its benefit is in the fact that it supports the development of a relevant purchasing strategy. If a strategy has been developed and decisions are still made without reference to the health needs assessment then it has been a waste of time. Development of the health needs assessment process must happen alongside a wider organizational development process and the training of senior decision makers within the health service on needs-based decision making.

The assessment of health need is therefore a strategic process. As such it is time-consuming. Many people seem to expect that health needs assessment will instantly provide answers to long-term and difficult operational issues, e.g. how to reduce long waiting lists in three weeks! Health needs assessment, given time, *will* provide the strategic background to focus and direct decision making but it will *not* provide all the answers to operational difficulties.

Obviously, decision making in the NHS is a complicated process and there will be many other strategic and political considerations which impinge on the relationship between assessment of health need, development of purchasing strategy and resource allocation. These should not prevent us from moving towards a more needs-based approach.

A FRAMEWORK FOR HEALTH NEEDS ASSESSMENT

Starting with the population rather than the present services is a daunting task unless there is some way to divide the population into meaningful groups. There are several ways of doing this. In the past *client groups* were the usual way. Client group based planning would look at special needs groups, such as the elderly, disabled people, mentally ill people, children and people with learning difficulties. Disease groups (e.g. diabetics) have also been used. Using either disease groups or client groups as a basis for a comprehensive population based assessment of health need causes problems, however. These are:

- there will be overlapping groups, e.g. elderly people with disabilities and diabetes;
- it excludes the needs of the majority of the population;
- it is likely to focus on users of services rather than all people in the community with the problem.

For these reasons another framework is needed to focus the health needs assessment process. The *life cycle framework* is the one we put forward in this book. There are several other approaches which could be used, such as client based approaches, disease group approaches or the locality approach. As already mentioned, in the first two it is difficult not to restrict the needs assessment process to already existing services and the current users. Preventive services and the need for services for people for whom the health service has traditionally had little to offer (e.g. older people with sight problems caused by age related macular degeneration) can be forgotten using these approaches.

Locality needs assessment is becoming quite popular. We examine it briefly in the next section before continuing the exposition of the life cycle framework. The two approaches are not incompatible but it will become apparent (especially in Chapter 5) that the life cycle framework is the more powerful starting point for needs assessment and that it can incorporate other perspectives.

Locality needs assessment

In locality needs assessment the population is divided into groups geographically. This approach identifies geographical variations in health and allows them to be related to other demographic and social variables, such as the proportion of people unemployed, the proportion of elderly people and various measures of social deprivation. Health resources can also be measured and correlated geographically, e.g. health centres, leisure centres, parks and housing type.

This is a very important process in exploring the geographical relationships within a district or FHSA and it can allow certain areas to be targeted for resource allocation. However, the local population must still be divided by age and gender in order to assess comprehensively their health needs. Even within one locality the needs of an eight-year-old are very different from those of an eighty-year-old. Traditional epidemiological measures, such as the SMR, years of life lost or life expectancy at birth, are not useful in small localities as the numbers of events are too small (see Chapter 3).

Locality needs assessment is different from *locality service coordination* (often known as locality planning). The latter is an operational management tool which is particularly useful for providers of services in the community to enable them to coordinate service provision across agencies. For this to happen most effectively the locality boundaries must be the same between different agencies, which is often not the case.

Why the life cycle framework?

Age (or stage in the *biological life cycle*) and gender are two of the main determinants of both health and the use of health services in a population. Unless these determinants are taken into account then making services or policies appropriate to the needs of the local population will not be possible.

What is the life cycle framework?

In this section we present a quick summary of the life cycle framework. More details of its rationale, structure and use are presented in Chapter 5.

The life cycle framework divides the population to be studied into nine life cycle stages from before birth to old age. From age 15 years, the life cycle stages are also subdivided by gender because after this age the health experience of women is significantly different from that of men.

Its value is that it takes into account the biological, psychological and social determinants of health. The life stages are chosen because they represent periods in people's lives when certain factors tend to predominate in determining their health experience. Thus the health of a woman between the ages of 25 and 44 years is likely to be influenced by her fertility and to be related very much to child-bearing and child-rearing. Men's health between the ages of 15 and 24 years is likely to be determined by their developing sexuality and their changing image of themselves as adults and consequently by an increased likelihood of involving themselves in behaviours detrimental to their health.

The nine life stages chosen are as follows.

1 Late pregnancy to one week after birth.
2 One week to one year.
3 One year to four years.
4 Five years to 14 years.
5 15 years to 24 years.
6 25 years to 44 years.

7 45 years to 64 years.
8 65 years to 74 years.
9 Over 74 years.

Dividing the community into a number of groups of people in life cycle stages takes into account the importance of age and gender in determining the health experience of a community. Age and gender are not the only influences on health, however. The framework therefore introduces 'modifiers'. These are factors known to influence the health experience of a community. In this book we explore socio-economic, environmental, ethnic and cultural influences on each of the life cycle groups.

The life cycle framework is a powerful tool for the assessment of health need in that it forces the needs of the whole population to be explored in a coherent way. It does not encourage health needs to be limited just to health service needs. The life cycle framework:

- forces detailed examination of the needs of differing groups in a coherent way;
- determines what information is required and does not force thinking to be constrained by what information currently happens to be available;
- allows the linking of information, planning and resource allocation in a more coherent way;
- allows health influences to be related to service provision either current or proposed, health service or non-health service, curative or preventive;
- explains rather than just describes the health of the community;
- easily accommodates any increase in our knowledge of the determinants of health and health service utilization in a population.

RELATIONSHIP OF THE LIFE CYCLE FRAMEWORK TO THE HEALTH FOR ALL PHILOSOPHY

In 1979, at the 34th World Health Assembly, the World Health Organization adopted as its goal *Health for All by the Year 2000* (HFA). In 1984 the European Region produced its strategy based on this goal.[7] This strategy was adopted by most governments of member states, including the UK government. It is a strategy for overall health improvement based on six major themes. These are quoted below.

1 Health for all implies *equity*. This means that the present inequalities in health between countries and within countries should be reduced as far as possible.
2 The aim is to give people a positive sense of health so that they can make full use of their physical, mental and emotional capacities. The

main emphasis should therefore be on *health promotion* and the pre-vention of disease.

3 Health for all will be achieved by people themselves. A well informed, well motivated and actively *participating community* is a key element for the attainment of the common goal.

4 Health for all requires the coordinated action of all sectors concerned. The health authorities can deal only with a part of the problems to be solved, and *multisectoral cooperation* is the only way of effectively en-suring the prerequisites for health, promoting healthy policies and reducing risks in the physical, economic and social environment.

5 The focus of the health care system should be on *primary health care* – meeting the basic health needs of each community through services provided as close as possible to where people live and work, readily accessible and acceptable to all, and based on full community participation.

6 Health problems transcend national frontiers. Pollution and trade in health-damaging products are obvious examples of problems whose solution requires *international cooperation.*

In order to meet the overall goal, 38 specific targets were formulated. These fall under six broad headings:

- Health for all in Europe by the year 2000 (12 targets).
- Lifestyles conducive to health (5 targets).
- Healthy environment (8 targets).
- Appropriate care (6 targets).
- Research for health for all (1 target).
- Health development support (6 targets).

As should be clear from these lists, the HFA approach is founded on in-volvement of local communities, collaboration between diverse agencies, a recognition of the key role of primary care and an emphasis on health promotion and disease prevention.

As already stated, health needs assessment will always have a value base. This value base can be the values of Health for All or any other value system accepted by the health authority. Each purchasing organ-ization needs to clarify the value-based criteria it will use to judge options for maximizing health gain.

Choosing the values of Health for All as the basis of our health needs assessment process means that we will choose to define health gain as that which reduces inequity in health. It means that we will involve local people in determining local health gain priorities, in defining health problems, in defining health resources and in the decision making processes of option appraisal. Using the life cycle framework highlights other values inherent in the Health for All philosophy such as the importance of multisectoral collaboration, by emphasizing the role of other agencies as health resources. It also emphasizes the importance of health promotion and the prevention of disease. The book also makes clear the pivotal role of primary health care in addressing a community's health needs. It can be seen that assessing health need using the life cycle framework is consistent with the Health for All philosophy. While we see merit in using the Health for All values, the life cycle framework can also be used with any other value base.

REFERENCES

1 Buchan, H., Muir Gray, J. A., Hill, A. and Coulter, A. (1990) Needs assessment made simple. *Health Service Journal*, **100**, 240–1.
2 Donaldson, C. and Mooney, G. (1991) Needs assessment, priority setting and contracts for health care: an economic view. HERU Discussion Paper, Health Economics Research Unit, Aberdeen.
3 Eskin, F. and Bull, A. (1991) Squaring a difficult circle. *Health Service Journal*, **101**, 16–19.
4 Stevens, A. and Gabbay, J. (1991) Needs assessment needs assessment. *Health Trends*, **23**(1), 20–3.
5 Stevens, A. (1990) Assessing health care needs. Department of Health Project Paper, June.
6 *Purchasing Intelligence*. National Health Service Management Executive report, October 1991.
7 WHO (1985) *Targets for Health for All. Targets in Support of the European Regional Strategy for Health for All*. Copenhagen: World Health Organization Regional Office for Europe.

3 / AN INTRODUCTION TO ESSENTIAL DEMOGRAPHIC AND EPIDEMIOLOGICAL CONCEPTS

Demography is defined as

The study of populations, especially with reference to size and density, fertility, mortality, growth, age distribution, migration, and vital statistics, and the interaction of all these with social and economic conditions.[1]

Epidemiology is defined as

Study of the distribution and determinants of health-related states or events in specified populations, and the application of this study to control of health problems.[1]

These are distinct disciplines but epidemiology is founded upon demography and for our purposes may be taken to include it.

Epidemiological understanding and skills are essential for the determination of health status and the assessment of health need. The biological life cycle framework (Chapter 5 and following chapters) draws heavily upon epidemiological concepts. This chapter introduces sufficient epidemiology to enable the reader to progress with confidence. It also serves as a ladder by which the reader may ascend to the more comprehensive texts suggested in the further reading list at the end of this book.

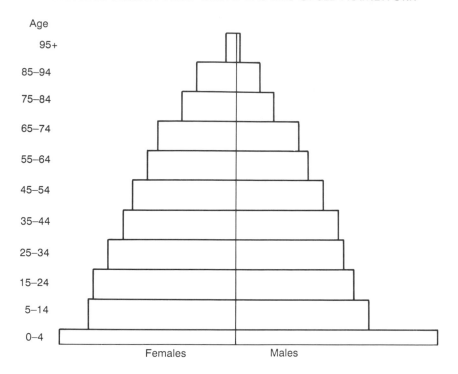

Age

Figure 3.1 A population pyramid: the age and gender structure of a population at a point in time. The area of each box is proportional to the size of the population it represents

THE POPULATION

Human populations are dynamic entities. Their compositions change with time under the influence of the prevailing birth rates, death rates and patterns of migration. At any point in time one may examine the structure and influences upon the population under study.

Figure 3.1 schematically displays a population pyramid. A population pyramid portrays a population divided into subgroups by age and gender. The area of each box is proportional to the size of the population in each subgroup. It should be noted that in developed countries these 'pyramids' are not strictly pyramidal; in the UK there is a marked bulge in the older age groups as a consequence of previous patterns of fertility and increasing longevity. Information on the size and gender structure of populations is available in most countries and in all developed countries.

Often, as in the UK, it is possible to obtain detailed information about relatively small geographically defined populations. The populations used in planning health and social services in the UK may be as small as the enumeration district (typically 500 in an urban area, see Glossary) but are more usually at the level of the electoral ward, health authority population, city or borough population, or some other convenient aggregate of smaller units. Many relevant sources of demographic information applicable to the UK are mentioned in Chapters 6 to 14 and an up-to-date and comprehensive summary of UK demographic and health information sources may be found in Appendices 3 and 4, and elsewhere.[2]

It should be borne in mind that a population pyramid is a snapshot of a changing entity. Leaving aside influences from immigration and emigration, the population pyramid can be considered to be like a snake. It 'eats' births at the base and gradually absorbs (through deaths) additions to the population as they pass through their lives. Thus a 'baby boom' such as occurred in the UK in the post Second World War years, manifests itself in many subsequent pyramids as a gradually decreasing bulge passing up the pyramids (a meal being digested by the snake). The rate of new entrants to the pyramid is determined by the number of people in their reproductive years and their propensity to reproduce; this latter is determined by myriad social and economic factors. The rate of 'digestion' of a cohort of births as they age is determined by the risks of dying prevailing as they enter each year of life. These age-specific risks (approximated by death rates – see below) change with time under the influence of social, economic and environmental factors, and through medical advance. However, the influence of medical advance may be less than is commonly supposed.[3]

From knowledge of the current size and structure of a population together with assumptions about future fertility, death rates and migration, predictions of future population size and composition can be made. In the UK these population estimates are fairly reliable for five, ten or perhaps fifteen years hence, but thereafter become increasingly suspect.

The age–gender structure of a population and its predicted change is fundamental to health needs assessment. In Chapter 5 we shall discuss how age (or stage in the biological life cycle) and gender influence health. The extent of health needs and the cost of meeting them are roughly proportional to the sizes of the age–gender groups under consideration. Moreover, the indices of health introduced in the remaining sections of this chapter require for their construction knowledge of the sizes of the populations potentially at risk.

THE INTERPRETATION OF INDICES OF MORBIDITY AND MORTALITY

This section explains some commonly used indices of mortality and morbidity. There is guidance on their interpretation and on how to avoid some pitfalls in their use.

Morbidity measures

Morbidity is ill-health. Morbidity ranges in severity from short-term self-limiting illness (e.g. the common cold) through chronic conditions that may be long-standing but are not necessarily lethal (e.g. rheumatoid arthritis) to fatal conditions (e.g. lung cancer). Two concepts are necessary for the description and an understanding of morbidity patterns in a population: incidence and prevalence.

Disease *incidence* measures the *rate of occurrence* of new cases of a disease in a defined population during a stated period of time, e.g. 15 cases per thousand population per year.

Disease *prevalence* measures the number of current cases of a particular disease present in a defined population during a defined period of time. In fact there are two possible measures: *point prevalence* and *period prevalence*. The former refers to a point in time or very short interval (days or a couple of weeks); the latter looks at the number of cases ever present during a longer period of time (weeks or months). Thus a point prevalence measure might be that there were 150 cases of a disease per thousand population on 2 July 1992, a period prevalence might be that there were 400 cases per thousand population during June to September 1992. Note that in a period prevalence measure individuals may be multiply counted if they have more than one distinct episode of the disease during the specified time interval.

A photographic analogy is helpful in understanding the difference between incidence and prevalence. A point prevalence ratio is akin to a flashlight still photograph of the population: it shows the burden of existing disease at a point in time. A period prevalence ratio is akin to a time-exposure photograph. An incidence rate summarizes what one would see if the flashlight photographs were strung together as a moving film: new (incident) cases of disease would arise in each frame.

Incidence rates are useful to planners because they show how many newly diagnosed cases of a disease to expect each year. Changes in incidence rates indicate that a disease is becoming a greater or lesser problem. Moreover, gradually decreasing incidence rates are a marker of success for health promotion and disease prevention strategies. Prevalence ratios indicate the burden of current disease, disability or handicap. These are particularly useful in identifying the health needs of the chronically ill.

There is a relationship between incidence and prevalence which is

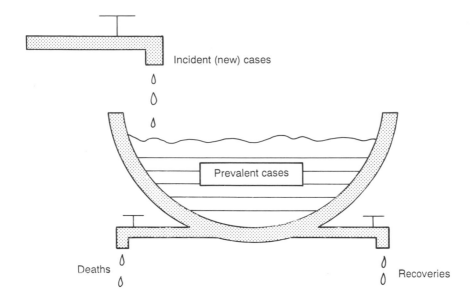

Figure 3.2 Epidemiology reduced to hydrodynamics· an illustration of the relationship between incidence, prevalence and the duration of disease

easily understood via another analogy. Consider a vessel into which water flows through a tap. At the base of the vessel are two outlets controlled by taps (see Figure 3.2). The level of water in the vessel (prevalence) will eventually reach an equilibrium dependent upon the rate of inflow (incident cases) and the rate of outflow (cases recovering or cases dying). If either of the outflows is increased and the inflow remains constant the level (prevalence) of water decreases to a new equilibrium; this is analogous either to medical advance leading to a shorter duration of disease or to the severity increasing and leading to more rapid deaths. If the inflow decreases and the overall outflow remains constant the water level will attain equilibrium at a lower level; this is analogous to a fall in disease incidence consequent upon health promotion, resulting in decreased disease prevalence. If the inflow remains constant and the overall outflow decreases the water level will rise; similarly the prevalence of a fatal disease will rise if treatment advances provide longer remission. The reader should work out possible reasons for, and the consequences of, the remaining possibilities.

Unfortunately, *very little* quantifiable and valid information about patterns of morbidity from non-fatal disease is available to the health service from routine information sources. Yet non-fatal disease accounts for the greater part of suffering in the population. It might be thought that service usage statistics (e.g. population rates of use of a particular service) can fill this gap. However, these are an unreliable source of information: usage is influenced by the availability of services and referral habits. Patterns of morbidity encountered in primary care are available from the few general practices having appropriate information systems; these too give a distorted picture of morbidity in the population at large, as much chronic and potentially treatable illness goes unrecognized because patients do not present themselves at surgeries.

Some information about incidence and prevalence can be gleaned from publications of specific studies and from a few specialized disease registers (e.g. cancer registries). Often information from studies conducted elsewhere can be applied in an *order of magnitude* manner to populations other than that studied. However, too much current service planning relies upon mortality statistics as proxies for morbidity.

There is a pressing need for family health service authority (FHSA) managers and their district health authority counterparts to explore means of improving routine information systems and to supplement information from routine systems by appropriate population screening studies. Indeed, the life cycle approach introduced later in this book helps to clarify those areas where more information is needed. Clearly, these are matters upon which guidance from public health physicians should be sought.

Mortality measures

Mortality by number and by cause has been reasonably accurately measured in the UK since the nineteenth century. Mortality statistics form the main basis of our understanding of how the health of the population has changed. Through incorporation into resource allocation formulae they considerably influence how health service funds are distributed geographically. Mortality statistics are presented in two general forms. First, death rates are simple estimates of the probability of someone in a defined population dying from a specific cause or group of causes during a specified time period. Second, summary statistics combine information from death rates to give easily digested overviews of the mortality experiences of populations. Examples of both will be presented.

The *crude annual death rate* for a population consists of the total number of deaths during a year divided by the size of the population. This is often, arbitrarily, multiplied by 1000 so that the rate can be stated as so many deaths per thousand, e.g. 11.4 per thousand. The top line of this division is known as the numerator and the bottom line the denominator. All the death rates presented below follow this basic pattern of a numerator consisting of the number of deaths and a denominator consisting of the population at risk of dying. Because all populations change through births, deaths and migration over the course of a year

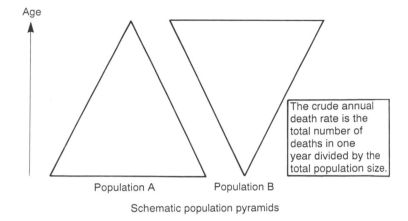

Figure 3.3   An illustration of how the crude death rate can mislead.
The populations are of equal size and the risk of dying in each age
group does not differ between the populations. However, population
B has the greater crude annual mortality rate, because it has the
greater proportion of old people, death rates are higher in the old,
and so there are more deaths in population B

there is difficulty in defining an unambiguous denominator population.
It is customary in official statistics to use an estimate of what the population was half-way through the year, i.e. the midyear population.

The crude death rate is literally so crude that it can be dangerously
misleading and it should never be used in health service planning. It is
tempting to use it as a summary of the mortality experience of an entire
population. However, if populations with different age structures (unlike
proportions of young, middle-aged and old people) are compared their
crude death rates are influenced by both the probability of dying at each
age and the age structure of the population. Populations with a preponderance of old people have higher crude death rates than populations
with a preponderance of young people even when the chance of dying
at each specific age is the same in both populations. This merely reflects
the fact that old people have a much greater biological risk of dying than
the young and that populations with a large proportion of old people are
unduly weighted by people with an age-determined risk of death. The
argument is illustrated in Figure 3.3. Legitimate summary statistics will
be presented below.

Age-specific death rates portray the chances of dying in defined age
groups. If the age bands are sufficiently narrow, e.g. five or ten years,
age-specific rates may be compared between populations with little risk

of the biases inherent in the crude death rate. The age-specific death rate in England for men aged 45–54 years in 1992 is defined as follows:

$$\frac{\text{number of men dying aged 45–54 years during 1992}}{\text{midyear 1992 male population aged 45–54 years}}$$

Customarily this will be multiplied by 100 000 and thus the death rate will be quoted as so many per 100 000 male population aged 45–54 years per year.

Age–cause-specific death rates are a simple extension of the foregoing. The numerator now refers to deaths from a specific cause or group of causes among the stated age group; the denominator is unchanged. Thus the age-specific death rate from coronary heart disease (CHD) among men in England aged 45–54 years in 1992 is:

$$\frac{\text{number of men aged 45–54 years in 1992 dying of CHD}}{\text{midyear 1992 male population aged 45–54 years}}$$

As before this is multiplied by 100 000.

Special mortality rates are defined for the very young. The two most commonly used are the *perinatal mortality rate* and the *infant mortality rate*. The *perinatal mortality rate* is defined as follows:

$$\frac{\text{number of stillbirths and deaths within 7 days of birth}}{\text{total number of live and stillborn babies}}$$

The numerator and the denominator each refer to deaths/births in a defined population during one year, e.g. the perinatal mortality rate for the resident population of South Manchester Health Authority in 1992. The rate is customarily multiplied by 1000 and thus quoted as so many (e.g. 11.4) deaths per thousand live births and stillbirths. The perinatal mortality rate (often abbreviated to PNMR) is a sensitive indicator of the quality of pregnancies, the care associated with delivery and events in the early days of life.

The *infant mortality rate* is defined thus:

$$\frac{\text{number of deaths of live born children under one year of age}}{\text{total number of live born babies}}$$

The numerator and denominator refer respectively to deaths and births in a *defined population* during *one year*. The rate is customarily multiplied by 1000. The infant mortality rate measures the risks to life during the first year and is less influenced by events during pregnancy and delivery than is the PNMR.

Summary mortality statistics

Two summary statistics will be presented. These are the standardized mortality ratio and expectation of life. The purpose of both is to give a simple summary of the overall mortality experience of a population in such a way as to avoid the pitfalls associated with the crude death rate. In order to compare the overall health experience of one population with another, summary statistics are important because in an examination of age-specific death rates it is too easy to become overwhelmed by detail and to lose sight of broad features.

Construction of the *standardized mortality ratio* (SMR) is very simple. Suppose that the SMR for the Stockport Health Authority resident population in 1992 is to be computed. A standard reference population is chosen, usually England and Wales. The age-specific death rates for England and Wales in 1992 are known (published by the Office of Population Censuses and Surveys). The age structure of Stockport HA is known from the previous census, with estimated adjustments for subsequent change (i.e. how many people in 1992 were aged less than one, 1–4, 5–9, 10–14 years etc.). The next step is to calculate how many deaths would have occurred in 1992 in Stockport if the people in Stockport in each age group had exactly the same risk of dying as did people in the corresponding age groups in England and Wales as a whole. Now, suppose that in a particular age group the England and Wales risk of dying (death rate) was 50 per 100 000 and that in Stockport there were 20 000 people in that age group. Then if that risk obtained in Stockport, 10 (i.e. (50/100 000) × 20 000) people in the age group would be expected to die. This calculation is done for each age group and the deaths are accumulated to give a total number of *expected* deaths for Stockport. The only other ingredient necessary for the SMR is the total number of deaths *observed* to occur in Stockport and this will be readily to hand. Thus the SMR is:

$$\frac{\text{observed number of deaths in 1992}}{\text{expected number of deaths in 1992}}$$

Usually the above ratio is multiplied by 100 and expressed as a percentage. An SMR of 100 per cent would imply that Stockport had the same overall mortality experience as England and Wales. An SMR below 100 per cent indicates a more favourable overall mortality experience, and an SMR in excess of 100 per cent indicates a less favourable mortality experience.

If similar calculations were done for Brighton, South Glamorgan and Sheffield Health Authorities the overall mortality experiences of each could be compared with the others and with England and Wales. Furthermore, the fact that the age structures of these populations differ would introduce no serious bias into the comparisons. Incidentally, when a comparison of SMRs shows that the mortality experience of one population differs from another it does not indicate how that difference arises: there may be a systematic difference in all ages and for all diseases or it may be particular ages or diseases that differ. To find out more it will be necessary to examine age-specific death rates in detail. (To find out why the difference occurs and to assess how to address it will require a whole range of information. This is the assessment of health need process.)

The SMR need not be calculated for the entire age range. SMRs for people aged less then 65 years are believed to give a better picture of potentially avoidable mortality than all-age SMRs. Furthermore, SMRs may be calculated for specific diseases, e.g. coronary heart disease, and by gender. Every ten years (following the census) the Registrar General publishes SMRs by disease and occupational group for England and Wales. When the occupational groups are aggregated into occupational social classes (a practice now abandoned) the consequent SMRs reveal much about the statistical association between social class and mortality.

The *expectation of life at birth* summarizes the mortality experience of a population. The calculation is conceptually simple but fiddly in practice. Suppose we are interested in Blackpool. We have for 1992 the age-specific death rates of the Blackpool population. In essence, one starts with a hypothetical cohort of births, say 1000, and asks what would happen to that cohort if it were followed up for many years. In the first year of their lives the cohort would be subject to the Blackpool 1992 risk of dying for children aged less than one year; there would be some loss through death. In the second year the survivors will be subject to the Blackpool 1992 risk of dying for persons aged 1–2 years. In the twentieth year of the cohort's life the survivors would be subject to the Blackpool 1992 risk of dying for persons aged 19–20 years, etc. The result will be a table showing the numbers in the cohort surviving to each age and from this the average length of life of members of the cohort can be calculated: this is the expectation of life from birth. Clearly, it is also possible to calculate the expectation of life, or average extra years lived, from any given age on the assumption that someone has survived to that age (e.g. the number of further years people aged 50 in the cohort might expect). Expectations of life may be compared between populations with differing age structures.

As a simple summary of *current* (e.g. 1992) mortality experience in a population the expectation of life at birth is useful and harmless. However, it is often misunderstood and abused. An expectation of life at birth computed for Blackpool in 1992 does not mean that children born in Blackpool in 1992 will live on average to that age. Indeed those children will in all probability have a considerably greater actual (and unknown) expectation of life because age-specific mortality has in all age groups been diminishing during this century and is likely to continue so to do. Furthermore, a low expectation of life at birth in one district, say North

Manchester, as compared to another, say Trafford, does not imply that North Manchester is a more risky place in which to live (although it may be). This is because the present mortality experience of people aged, say, 55 years does not reflect only current environmental and social circumstances. Each individual carries, as he or she passes from age group to age group, a baggage of previous experiences and accumulating risks. Some people aged 55 years may have smoked cigarettes for 40 years or may have worked in an environmentally polluted setting, whereas people born now in either North Manchester or Trafford may be subjected to considerably lesser risks as they progress through life. These caveats about over-interpreting expectation of life apply equally to comparisons between SMRs.

Mortality as a proxy for morbidity

In some limited circumstances mortality statistics may be used as a valid proxy for morbidity statistics. Diseases for which this is applicable are:

- those where case-fatality is high;
- those where case fatality remains fairly constant over a period of years;
- those where the duration of illness is fairly short, i.e. months or a few years but not decades.

For example, death rates are:

- excellent proxies for morbidity from lung cancer and pancreatic cancer;
- reasonable proxies for morbidity from coronary heart disease and breast cancer;
- poor proxies for morbidity from asthma and chronic bronchitis;
- hopeless proxies for morbidity from the common cold, whooping cough, rheumatoid arthritis, multiple sclerosis and hernias.

The paucity of true morbidity measures has led many health service planners and those responsible for resource allocation to use mortality statistics *merely because they are there*. In so far as justification is produced this is on the lines that when mortality is high then so generally is morbidity. This may be true but there is no known quantitative link between overall mortality and, for example, coronary heart disease morbidity, morbidity from rheumatoid arthritis or morbidity from asthma. Moreover, as mentioned above, current patterns of mortality may give a very poor picture of the present health risks of living in a particular community. It is also not widely appreciated that reductions in mortality from many diseases (e.g. cystic fibrosis) may bring about *increases* in morbidity because more chronically sick people will remain alive in the community. Certainly, mortality statistics are of very limited use in helping to decide which services to purchase to meet the as yet poorly quantified and often undramatic health needs of most communities.

COHORT ANALYSIS

The issues raised at the end of the preceding section lead us to consider the powerful epidemiological technique known as *cohort analysis*. Thus far, on several occasions, we have used the term cohort to denote a group of people followed over time. Specifically, we shall use the following definition of a *birth cohort*.

> The component of the population born during a particular period and identified by period of birth so that its characteristics (e.g. causes of death and numbers still living) can be ascertained as it enters successive time and age periods.[1]

It is useful to disentangle three kinds of influence on the health experiences of a birth cohort. The first is known as the *cohort effect*. This is the consequence for health of the historical circumstances (social, economic, environmental etc.) into which the cohort was born. As time passes members of the cohort will be at a unique (as compared to other birth cohorts) biological age in each calendar year and may respond to those circumstances in a unique way influenced by their previous experiences.

Period effects refer to the influences on the health experiences of a cohort by events occurring at particular points in calendar time. Such events include wars, famines, pestilence and environmental disasters such as that at Chernobyl. A period effect may influence differing birth cohorts in differing ways. For example, the cohort born in 1940 is much less likely to be affected by an outbreak of pertussis (whooping cough) in 1992 than one born in 1990. This is illustrated in Figure 3.4.

The third influence is called the *age effect*. Biological age is a major determinant of health experience. Thus, regardless of the cohort effects or period effects, all birth cohorts when viewed at the same age (obviously they will not be at the same calendar time) have much in common. The age effect corresponds closely to our notion of the biological life cycle and is discussed in more detail in Chapter 5.

CLASSIFYING DISEASE

When attempting to quantify the burden of disease in a population and perhaps to compare it with the burden elsewhere, or at a different time, two problems emerge. First, nomenclatures of disease may differ in time and place, or, if standardized, may be applied by different clinicians in

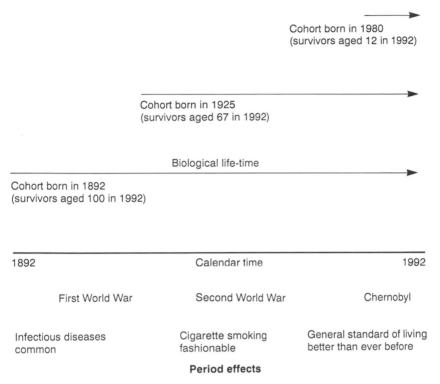

Figure 3.4   Cohort analysis: an illustration of the differing influences on the health of various birth cohorts present in 1992

idiosyncratic ways. Second, a means is required to code diagnostic information ready for its further use in morbidity and mortality statistics.

The International Classification of Disease (ICD) assists in both problems and is used routinely within the health service as well as by researchers. Although it is a classification and not a nomenclature, it nevertheless helps to iron out problems caused by differing fashions in diagnosis. This is because the classification can be used at many levels of detail, ranging from what at the lowest level is often a single diagnosis upwards to ever wider groupings of diagnoses. Thus a prudent choice of classification grouping will include sub-classifications, among which there is a possibility that a disease could have been misplaced. Because the classification is hierarchical and represented numerically it is ideally suited for processing on computers.

A closely related classification system that appears to be better suited to the information requirements of primary care has been introduced by Read.[4] Copyright for this has been purchased by the National Health Service. The classification covers all major areas relating to practice, from aetiology of disease through symptoms and signs to treatment of disease by medical and surgical means. It is a hierarchical system with, at present, five levels. Text terms are associated with an alphanumeric (letters and numbers) code. In contrast to ICD, where there are at each level ten options (the digits 0 to 9), the Read system, which uses upper and lower case letters, can produce 52 options. With the five digit code that is currently in use there are over 600 million possible final items, so that the system has a lot of reserve capacity. Read codes and ICD9 codes can be cross-referenced.

When information systems are interrogated for data about patterns of disease, both medical knowledge and familiarity with the ICD and Read classifications are desirable. Assistance in this should be forthcoming from public health physicians and others.

STATISTICAL ISSUES

A number of miscellaneous statistical issues will be discussed. They have been selected because they are the commonest reasons why health data are misinterpreted.

The definitions of *numerators* and *denominators* (i.e. the top and bottom lines in the divisions done to create ratios, rates and proportions) sometimes pose problems in screening programmes designed to find out the prevalence of disease. The numerator of a prevalence ratio must always be a subset of the denominator. Moreover, there must be strict and objective diagnostic criteria by which an individual may be included in the numerator. The denominator population must also be clearly defined in time and place and fully enumerated: it may be a geographical population (e.g. an electoral ward), a service defined population (e.g. a GP's practice list) or an institutionally defined population (e.g. elderly persons' homes). In addition, steps must be taken to ensure that every member of the denominator population who might be eligible for inclusion in the numerator is identified. This is particularly important in survey work that relies on cooperation from the public.

Suppose, for example, that elderly people on a practice list are to be screened to ascertain the prevalence of a variety of physical disabilities. The first problem is the definition of elderly people; let us assume that these are taken to be those aged 70 years or above on 1 January 1992. The second problem is the accuracy and completeness of the practice list; some old people may still be on the list although they have died or moved away. The third problem is the definition of disease and disability; this is particularly important if the examinations are to be done by more than one person and if the findings are to be compared with those from elsewhere. The fourth problem concerns how the screening will take place. If the elderly people are invited to attend the surgery for examination a substantial proportion are likely not to respond. If the disease and disability prevalence ratios are computed on the basis of those who did respond it is very likely that these ratios will be an underestimate of the true prevalences, the reason being that some of the non-responders were people who by virtue of their disabilities could not easily attend the surgery.

In surveys where the potential denominator population is very large it is customary to look at samples of the population rather than the whole of it. There are many pitfalls for the unwary in sampling. Advice should be sought from a public health physician or statistician.

When service usage data (e.g. Körner episodes) are being examined in an attempt to assess need or demand it is important to distinguish between *people* and *episodes*. A person treated twice for the same disease will count as two episodes. This is fine for assessing workload but may be unhelpful in an attempt to compute incidence. With information systems designed to link patient records between stays in hospital it is easy to distinguish people from episodes. With purely episode based systems it is possible by extremely tedious manual methods to link records on the basis of patient identifiers.

When statistics (e.g. death rates) that are known to have been computed properly and with due regard to the definition of numerators and denominators are available there remains the problem of whether they should be taken at face value. If the numerator is substantial and the denominator is very large, as is the case with national or regional statistics, then generally they can. However, when statistics are presented for district health authority resident populations or for sub-populations within authority boundaries problems may arise. Suppose that year by year the risk of stillbirth or death within the first year of life remains constant and that each year the perinatal mortality rate (PNMR) is computed. Each year the observed PNMR would differ but it would fluctuate around an average that is the true underlying risk. For a large population of births (e.g. England and Wales) these fluctuations would be very small. For the births arising within the resident population of a health authority they would be substantial. Let us explore this with some numbers.

Suppose that the number of births (live and still) is 2000 and constant year by year. Also suppose that the *average* number of stillbirths and deaths in the first week of life is 30. Then the constant underlying PNMR is 15 per thousand live births and stillbirths. It can be shown by statistical calculation that if the PNMR is calculated year by year it will be found to fluctuate such that on 95 per cent of occasions it lies between 10.1 per 1000 and 21.4 per 1000. On 5 per cent of occasions it will be more extreme.

Now suppose that we are looking at a group of wards which make up half the district and that the underlying risk is the same. The number of births will be 1000 and the average number of deaths will be 15. The PNMR will on 95 per cent of occasions lie between 8.4 per 1000 and 24.7

per 1000. If we halve the population yet again the PNMR will range between 6.3 per 1000 and 30.1 per 1000 even though the *underlying risk of death is constant*. Clearly, in circumstances where the PNMR is expected to fluctuate from year to year even if the risk of death is not changing, it would be imprudent of planners to draw far-reaching conclusions from moderate changes in the PNMR from that of the previous year.

Everything that has been illustrated with the PNMR applies to incidence rates, prevalence ratios, age-specific death rates, the standardized mortality ratio and expectation of life. The likelihood of these fluctuations being due to chance depends upon how common the condition under study is in the population being examined. Thus coronary heart disease SMRs for a single year can be looked at with some confidence on a district basis but they become prone to considerable fluctuation at electoral ward level; testicular cancer SMRs cannot be looked at reliably even at district level.

Two strategies help when one is faced with the small numbers problem. The first is to aggregate data for small populations over a period of years (say five or ten). This stabilizes the rates or SMRs but has the disadvantage of obscuring information about trends in time. The second technique is to plot the time trend and smooth out fluctuations using moving averages; that is, the point plotted for each year might be the average of the actual value for that year together with the actual values for the preceding year and following year. In essence, however, small numbers mean that there is little information with which to play and no amount of statistical sophistication can create new information; statistics can only help to present what there is to best advantage. Advice from public health physicians and statisticians should be sought on these matters.

The final issue to be discussed is that of imputing *causal relationships*. The literature abounds with studies that show statistical associations between life-style factors, environmental agents, health service interventions and the propensity for disease. To show such associations is easy, but to justify a statement that one factor causes the outcome is very difficult. In general such statements can only be proved by conducting rigorous experimental trials. Unfortunately, in many instances such trials are impracticable either because of their cost and time-scale or because of ethical reasons. Therefore, much of the evidence that is used to justify various assertions is less than perfect and in consequence always open to challenge. Nevertheless, decisions have to be taken and there are general principles that assist in assessing the plausibility of causality from circumstantial evidence. These principles, based on those enunciated by Sir Austin Bradford Hill,[5] are:

1 The plausibility of the assertion of causality. That is, whether the assertion and the proposed mechanism of causality are consistent with

current knowledge of the biology of human beings and of their environmental circumstances and social behaviour.

2 The assumed cause must be demonstrated to precede rather than follow the supposed effect.

3 Coherence of evidence from different sources and different kinds of study, and where there is inconsistency a plausible explanation for it.

4 The assumed cause is specific in its effects.

5 The strength of the association, e.g. as represented by the magnitude of statistical measures of association.

6 Presence of a dose–response relationship. That is, if the degree of exposure to a causal agent can be quantified then one usually expects to find a greater effect or response for greater exposures to the agent.

7 Intervening (i.e. an experiment) to change the assumed cause leads to a corresponding change in the outcome.

REFERENCES

1 Last, M. L. (ed.) (1988) *A Dictionary of Epidemiology*. Oxford: Oxford University Press.

2 St Leger, A. S., Schnieden, H. and Walsworth-Bell, J. P. (1992) *Evaluating Health Services' Effectiveness – a Guide for Health Professionals, Service Managers and Policy Makers*. Buckingham: Open University Press, Chapter 4 and Appendix A.

3 McKeown, T. (1976) *The Role of Medicine – Dream, Mirage or Nemesis?* London: The Nuffield Provincial Hospitals Trust.

4 Read, J. D. (1990) Computerising medical language. *British Journal of Health Care Computing*, Conference Proceedings, **HC90**, 203–8.

5 Hill, A. B. (1977) *A Short Textbook of Medical Statistics*. London: Hodder and Stoughton.

4 / SOCIOLOGICAL APPROACHES TO COLLECTING INFORMATION ON HEALTH NEEDS*

INTRODUCTION

The concept of need is not generally recognized as one of the core ideas of sociology. Most of the research on need that has emerged in the past twenty years or so has come from philosophers and experts in social policy, often in the context of more general treatises on the nature of justice or the organization of the welfare state.[1] However, the concept of need is clearly a sociological one in so far as it is used to characterize situations in terms of both personal troubles – the experiences that human beings have – and public issues – the situations within which those experiences are framed. It is this sociological perspective that has under-pinned much of the writing on need in the social sciences and humanities. Researchers have spent a great deal of time naming needs, conceptual-izing needs and measuring needs, all the time trying to keep sight of the fact that need, although it is something an individual may be said to feel or express, is not a property of individuals but rather an expression of their relationship to other individuals and to society.[2]

* The authors are greatly indebted to Jennie Popay and Gareth Williams for writing this chapter. The section on Rapid Appraisal was written by Bie Nio Ong and edited by Popay and Williams.

Research on 'need' has a relatively short history. Before the establishment of the welfare state in Britain after the Second World War need was scarcely spoken about in academic circles; and it is only in the past fifteen years or so that 'needology' has become an identifiable subset of academic activity.[3] The welfare state provided the justification for the definition of certain things as needs and for the formalization of these needs as entitlements. It also legitimated the right of certain occupational groups to represent the needs of people they did not know personally – the needs of strangers. Within the resurgent free market ideology need has been used as the basis for rationing rather than as a principle of redistribution. The most recent discourses on need have arisen in response to the crisis of the welfare state and the assault on its basic premises and organizational arrangements. This crisis is at root a fiscal crisis, but it is also a crisis of belief – a crisis of legitimacy in a society that draws a heavy line between those who 'work' and those who do not, between those who are independent and those who are dependent, between those who are self-supporting and those who are in need of support.[4]

This brief statement indicates the potential difficulties involved in collecting information on health needs. The need for health and health care is now seen as one of the basic needs of people living in societies with established welfare states. However, the current renewed concern about 'health needs assessment' stems from the conjunction of three developments: concern about the exponential growth of public expenditure, recognition of the implications of an ageing population, and continuing high expectations about health care. Contrary to the hopes invested in the NHS at its inception, health services do not reduce the pool of illness in society. Through studies of illness behaviour and health service utilization we now understand ill-health, and the need for health care, as something much more complicated than was first thought; and with the rise of chronic disease as the major public health problem, health care in general and the NHS in particular are expected to do many more things than was first envisaged.[5]

As soon as we move away from the standard indicators of mortality and health service use as proxy measures of need – as we must if we are to make health services responsive to population needs – we confront the problem of how to find out what people's needs are. Even if one accepts the narrow definition of need as 'the ability to benefit from' services, sociological perspectives illuminate the fact that ability to benefit depends critically on the situation in which needs are created and perceptions of them framed.

What we have said here indicates that finding out about what people need to promote and care for their health and to treat ill-health involves more than asking individuals to list frequency of symptoms or the extent of their mobility problems. Communicating one's needs involves more than expressing a preference in response to questions in a survey; and health needs are more than what health care professionals think people ought to have. It is something requiring an approach to the collection of data that encompasses a recognition of the social basis of health needs, and a respect for what people themselves have got to say – an interest, that is, in lay as well as clinical epidemiology. Traditional research approaches to collecting information simply cannot match up to these requirements. The nature of the research questions posed by a sociological perspective on needs requires what one prominent medical sociologist has typified as methods that encourage hard thinking about soft issues – the methods of qualitative research.

QUALITATIVE SOCIOLOGICAL RESEARCH AND THE PURCHASING AGENDA

Making health services more responsive to the needs, views and preferences of local people is central to the new role of DHAs and FHSAs. At the present time a great deal of thought is being given to how purchasers can find out about these needs, views and preferences and how they can establish and maintain a dialogue with local people. There will be several related dimensions to the strategies that are adopted, but research will play a crucial role. This research must move beyond the traditional survey – much more emphasis should be given to the contribution of qualitative sociological research.

What is qualitative sociological research?

Much is made of the difference between qualitative and quantitative research but it is difficult to draw a hard and fast distinction between the two.[6] Moreover, people have sometimes seemed so obsessed with seeing the matter as one of either/or that it has led them to forget that the methods used should depend on the questions asked in response to a problem, not the other way around.

In general, qualitative research produces *non-numerical* information. A primary objective of such research is to understand the *meaning* that people give to their experiences and behaviour through the study of words, images and actions. While quantitative approaches emphasize standardization in data collection, those engaged in using qualitative methods allow the nature of the questions they ask or the observations they make to vary from one setting to another. Doing qualitative research is not simply a matter of using different research methods. Indeed, to some extent, the same research methods can provide either qualitative or quantitative data. Nothing is inherently qualitative or quantitative.

Words, images, actions and texts, which can give some understanding of the meanings that people attach to their experiences and behaviour, can also be transformed into quantitative terms and used as the basis for different levels of measurement.

Qualitative research is a different kind of research process from that associated with quantitative research. It has different objectives, asks different kinds of questions and provides different kinds of answers. Quantitative research will tell you how many people smoke in your district; qualitative research will give you an understanding of why they continue to do so even though they know it is damaging their health. Quantitative research will tell you how many people suffer from chronic diseases and disabilities; qualitative research will tell you what it means to people to be disabled and show the myriad ways in which it affects their daily lives. Quantitative research will tell you how many people in a locality 'need' different kinds of services; a qualitative approach will give you a sense of the range of health needs in a locality and the strength of feelings about different issues.

Qualitative research provides rich pictures of the concerns and pre-occupations of people in their everyday lives. Findings can be presented back to participants in a way they will themselves understand, and their comments can be incorporated in the final report.

The role of qualitative research in purchasing

Qualitative research has a unique contribution to make in involving local people in the purchasing process within the NHS. There are three main reasons for this. First, it gives priority to the perceptions of the people being researched. It seeks to see the world as others see it in order to understand better why people think and act in the ways they do. Second, it involves a flexible approach to research. The nature of the research design, the sample and the topics to be covered can be amended during the research process in the light of preliminary findings. Qualitative research is therefore able to identify and describe the perspectives of local people on health needs and on how these can be met, and it can be finely tuned to the concerns of purchasers. Finally, qualitative research seeks the active participation of the research subjects. It is not therefore simply a way of collecting particular types of information for purchasing. It is also a means by which local people can feel actively involved in the purchasing process rather than being seen as the passive providers of information.

Qualitative research is not new to the NHS. Many purchasers have already commissioned such research to assess health and health care needs. One study, for example, is considering the needs of people with an addiction problem using in-depth interviews with a small number of service users and providers. Other studies involve the use of group interviews or focus groups, to elicit the preferences of people on a range of health issues and to get a sense of their priorities.

More generally, purchasers are involved in activities designed to allow local people to express their needs and priorities in their own way. Purchasing authorities, for example, are involved in extensive consultation exercises in the development of community care plans; have organized public meetings to discuss their new role with local communities; have been systematically visiting local groups; have undertaken rapid appraisal or scanning exercises to assess health needs in small localities; and are working with local communities using a community development model. These activities may be undertaken for a variety of reasons but they can be a source of rich qualitative information.

Despite these examples, it is clear that qualitative research could be used much more extensively by NHS purchasers to obtain the views of local people and to involve them in the purchasing process. However, if this potential is to be tapped effectively purchasers need to:

- understand what kind of information is generated by qualitative research;
- know when qualitative research is most appropriately used;
- be aware of the range of research methods that are available for obtaining qualitative data;
- ask the right questions when commissioning qualitative research;
- know where to go to find out more about qualitative research.

Standards in qualitative research

Within the NHS, people are often involved in interpreting and assessing quantitative information. The focus here is normally on issues such as validity and reliability. Is the sample representative? How can we be sure that there was no bias in the collection of the data? Is the information collected reliable? How do we know that the interpretations of the data are valid? Can the results of this study be generalized to other cases or situations? Although similar questions can be asked of qualitative research, the answers one is looking for to assess the standard of the data provided will be very different. Qualitative research has to be assessed in terms of what it sets out to do. There are important technical considerations related to sampling and to questions of reliability, validity and scope to generalize but these are not the same as those associated with quantitative research.

Sampling

One of the limitations often raised in connection with qualitative research is that the findings cannot be generalized because the sources of data – a case study or a small number of interviews or observations – are not representative. In some instances, however, it is perfectly appropriate to generalize from such research. In part it depends on the focus. To the extent that qualitative research elucidates processes the findings can be generalized beyond the people or organizations involved. Qualitative work on the relationship between women's smoking behaviour and poverty, for example, has wide applicability. Even when some aspects of the findings are correctly defined as particular to the case being studied (the views of people in a small locality, for example), the relationship between these views and factors such as class, gender and race is likely to transcend the boundaries of the community in question.

The use of the random sample in quantitative studies is based on assumptions about the probability that the characteristics found in the sample will also exist in the wider population from which it is drawn. There is no reason why this procedure cannot also be used to ensure the representativeness of individuals selected as respondents within case studies. While the selection of a case study – a particular hospital or a community group – may be necessarily non-random, the selection of respondents within that case study can be random.

When the focus of the research is to gain insight into what a neighbourhood or voluntary association feels and thinks about health needs and health services, random or probability sampling may be neither efficient nor effective. In exploratory qualitative research, sampling of any sort before the initiation of the research may be impossible. The researcher may have no more than rough guidelines about the kinds of people it might be useful to interview or observe in a given case. The logical justification for selection of respondents or informants is something that is only done afterwards, *post hoc*. It is right that we should feel uncomfortable about this, and insist that further, more systematic studies be undertaken afterwards.

In addition to exploratory work, there are other situations in qualitative research in which probability sampling may not be relevant to the kinds of questions being asked or the kinds of problems being unravelled. Non-random sampling will then be used. There are three forms of non-random sampling.

Quota sampling, which is also used in survey research, involves the prior determination of the categories of subjects the researcher wishes to observe or interview, such as age groups or people with a particular illness. A specified number of people within each of these categories will then be selected. Having done this, the researcher may modify or add to these categories and sample from these, a process which can then recur a number of times.

Snowball sampling is a process whereby the researcher will begin by interviewing one or two members of, say, a housing estate and then generate further respondents by asking these first respondents to give the names of other people who might be willing and able to talk about the topic of the research. This method is particularly useful for generating a 'community sample'.

Theoretical or *purposive sampling* is the third approach. Here the selection of cases, informants or situations is geared to the generation of conceptual or theoretical categories. The procedure involves first selecting apparently similar cases to build up an understanding of a particular issue, and then searching for exceptions or critical cases that might challenge the analysis being developed. In other words, the researcher uses a series of cases that attempt both to build up an explanation for something and to falsify it.

Reliability

In quantitative research reliability refers to the degree of consistency with which instances are assigned to the same category by different observers or by the same observer on different occasions. This issue is central when assessing the standard of quantitative data. However, in qualitative research the issue of reliability takes on a different meaning.

It is possible when doing observational work, for example, or coding transcripts of unstructured interviews, to compare the coding of two or more people. However, within such comparison the result will not be the computing of a coefficient of reliability, but rather a dialogue on the different interpretations being made. In some ways therefore this will be of more relevance to concerns about validity.

Validity

The question of validity lies at the heart of all scientific research. It is concerned with truth, although, as Bertrand Russell noted, all science is concerned with approximations to the truth. A description, explanation or account is valid if it represents accurately those features of the phenomena that it is intended to describe or explain. There are many different types of validity: face validity, convergent validity, discriminant validity and so on. However, the ultimate concern of the researcher is always with 'construct validity': the validity of the lines of inference running between data and concepts.

In the context of a survey construct validity refers to 'the extent to which the measurement corresponds to theoretical concepts (constructs) concerning the phenomenon under study'.[7] Is the mortality rate in a local community, for example, a 'valid' proxy for the health status of that community (see the discussion in Chapter 3)? In survey research it is customary to hear people talking of survey questions as items that have been 'well validated'. What this means is that they have been used in a variety of different contexts, and have been shown to be good indicators of the particular concept of interest.

The problem of validity is different within qualitative research. Rather than a concern with finding a precise indicator for a concept in advance of the research, there is a continuous interplay between finding indicators and developing concepts. Qualitative research would, for example, be concerned to identify and describe what 'being healthy' or 'being ill' means to people in a local community – the issue is how they define it.

WHEN TO USE QUALITATIVE RESEARCH

In the purchasing process there will be many instances when the primary aim is to *measure* health care needs. However, there may be insufficient information on which to base the production of a standardized questionnaire. Quantitative research therefore has to be preceded by an exploratory stage based on qualitative research. The objective here might be to identify the range of topics to be covered in a questionnaire or the dimensions to be included in a particular scale. Alternatively qualitative research may be used to pilot the instruments to be used in quantitative research. Although it is preliminary, the information generated by these activities can be of direct use to purchasers.

Reaching the parts other research cannot reach

In some instances there will be a strong case for undertaking qualitative research as a complement to quantitative research. Qualitative information may, for example, illuminate confusing aspects of a numerical picture. In a health survey, for example, it is not uncommon to find that a significant proportion of people report a serious disabling condition yet report no contact with health services. To understand why this is the case and the extent to which it represents unmet need qualitative research will be necessary. Qualitative research can also be used to add depth to the bare statistical bones of numerical information. Bringing findings to life in this way can often contribute to the more effective use of research within organizations.

There are also instances when the subject of interest is simply not amenable to quantification. A particularly topical example of this relates to our understanding of the prevalence and transmission of HIV and AIDS. This topic combines many features that can indicate the need to employ qualitative methods. First, it is a *sensitive topic*, on which people may not be willing to fill in questionnaires, even if they are confidential. Second, questionnaires may not be readily devised to cover the *complexity* of the interest. Third, and perhaps most importantly, the *research population will be difficult to locate* and therefore not amenable to a survey. Finally, such a study needs to focus on *relationships and interaction*.

These characteristics, sensitivity, complexity, invisibility and a focus on relationships and interaction, are not confined to topics such as HIV and AIDS.[8] The health needs and priorities of less articulate groups in a community, for example, or of minority groups, may be best researched through qualitative methods.

Facilitating action and evaluating change

Qualitative techniques are well suited when the primary objective of the research is to facilitate action. Research involving qualitative techniques could aid an understanding of the processes contributing to a low take-up of preventive services, for example, while also facilitating a dialogue with local people about how to change things. Testing the response of local people to proposals for service changes can also be an integral part of the design of qualitative research, providing an opportunity for these to be discussed and amended before implementation. The evaluation of policy initiatives can also involve qualitative research, particularly when the focus is on understanding why an initiative succeeds or fails rather than on measuring the impact or outcome of an initiative.

TECHNIQUES IN QUALITATIVE RESEARCH

Qualitative information can be collected in many different ways. Hospital architecture and art forms, for example, have been rewarding areas for study, telling us much about how societies have viewed sickness in the past. However, there are four research methods that are commonly used to obtain qualitative data:

- observation (non-participant and participant);
- informal interviewing;
- group interviewing and focus groups;
- document analysis.

Observation

Observation[9] is perhaps the first step in all scientific activity. It includes what you see, hear, smell and taste. The smell of a hospital ward, the image of an inner-city area, or the atmosphere of a hospital casualty area, may tell a researcher more about needs than all the interviews in the world.

Observation is normally undertaken in naturally occurring situations, in contrast to the artificial settings of interviews. However, it can be difficult to move from the everyday observation and perception that we all do to the more systematic activity that we characterize as science, particularly if one is observing the familiar. Much of our daily lives is spent in routines that we take for granted and do not analyse. Yet these everyday aspects of life are often of importance from a health perspective. Researchers therefore have to take particular care not to neglect everyday aspects of the things they are observing.

Observation can be participant or non-participant, though this distinction is not rigid. Participant observation involves 'living another's life' for a while and therefore reduces the problem associated with trying to observe the familiar. Many more aspects of a 'borrowed' life are likely to appear strange to the participant observer, so becoming more visible.

The most common criticism of observation based research is that the presence of the observer will have an effect on what is being observed. Most managers will know of the Hawthorn effect, which was seen when the workers in the Hawthorn factory in America changed their behaviour because they were being experimented on. However, observation, whether participant or not, does differ in an important respect from experimentation in that no attempt is made to modify what people are doing. It can also be less obtrusive, particularly if conducted over a lengthy period of time. Observation work has been widely used within health research. There have been observation based studies of medical practice, including surgery. One recent study of hospital catering staff provided valuable insights into how different patients were labelled and treated. There have also been a large number of studies of local communities that have involved observational work.

Interviewing

The most common method for collecting qualitative information about people's views on health and health care needs, and how to meet these, is by talking to them in a one-to-one interview.[10] Obviously, interviews can be used to obtain quantitative data but the interview in qualitative research is different in several crucial respects.

In qualitative research the interview takes the form of a 'guided conversation'. Informality is the key feature of these interviews and, ideally, the researcher allows the person being interviewed to talk at length. Often there is no set list of questions to be asked, merely a set of topics that can be explored as and when it seems appropriate. These interviews generate a considerable amount of information and they are commonly taped, although some researchers prefer to take notes.

The interviewer seeks to understand the informant's world-view by raising topics of interest, but allowing the form the response takes to be determined by the respondent. The focus is not necessarily on the frequency with which things are said but rather on trying to get people to reflect on issues and to reveal more than they would perhaps normally do. The informal interview is therefore designed to explore themes and ideas. It is ideal for investigating the subtle, the complex and the controversial, as well as the unknown.

A distinction is often made between *structured, semi-structured* and *unstructured* interviews. In fact, this distinction is not particularly helpful as all interviews are structured to some extent by the parties involved. In practice what often happens is that the interviewing will start almost completely unstructured, and as themes emerge these will be incorporated into a guide. In this way the interview may gradually move towards the semi-structured and then the structured.

It is often argued that informal interview data are particularly unreliable. They are characteristically personal and engaged, and a series of informal interviews in the same study will often cover very different terrains. However, this does not necessarily mean that unstructured interviews produce more biased data than structured or standardized interviews, simply that they produce different kinds of data. In emphasizing the non-directive nature of the encounter, and in focusing on listening rather than asking questions, such interviews can provide a valid account of the respondent's reality. For this reason, they have been said to be less biased than standardized interviews.

All interview data should be viewed with some suspicion. In any interview people may simply say what they think the questioner wants to hear or they may not have an opinion on something until asked about it. Either way, the data collected will be an artefact – created by the method of investigation itself. More importantly, the most common mistake in interview based research is to assume that the data reveal people's behaviour directly, when they are simply a potentially unreliable report on that behaviour.

Although the informal interview in qualitative research is often described as 'a conversation', this does not mean that anyone can conduct one. The success of such interviews depends upon the ability to ask the right question at the right time, to know when to listen and when to speak, to know how to be non-threatening and supportive, how to communicate non-verbally as well as verbally. The researcher must encourage interviewees to talk freely about themselves in order to improve the quality and validity of the information.

Group interviews and focus groups

Group interviews[11] are a common feature of qualitative research. They make use of group dynamics in order to produce information on attitudes, perceptions, beliefs and predispositions. They may also be used to try out and generate ideas. The main advantages of group interviews are that they:

- allow for greater numbers of respondents to be 'sampled' in a shorter time frame;
- may make the interview less strange and stressful than one-to-one interviews;

- provide a social context for people's responses, which can contribute to change when the research is action-oriented;
- provide a stimulus for people's ideas, something for people to react to, so avoiding monosyllabic responses.

Group interviews cost less per informant than individual interviews. However, it is important that the choice of this technique is not shaped by this consideration alone. False economies will result if the technique is inappropriately used.

There are definite disadvantages to group interviewing. Social pressures within the group may constrain some people from speaking freely. For obvious reasons groups do not produce reliable information on levels of awareness and knowledge. The information obtained may have less depth than that obtained via informal interviews, though this may be compensated for by the range of issues that can be covered.

Focus groups constitute one specific technique within the broader category of group interviewing. The technique has been developed and used extensively in research aimed at the marketing of particular products. The hallmark of focus groups 'is the explicit use of group interaction to produce data and insights that would be less accessible without the interaction found in the group'.[11] Focus groups work well where there are stimulus materials both to open up and to focus the discussions among group members; hence their widespread use within market research. They can provide rich qualitative information on why people think and feel the ways they do.

Typically a focus group consists of seven to ten participants who are unfamiliar with each other but who share certain characteristics relevant to the topic, such as age, sex, parental or marital status. The aim is to create a permissive environment in which group members can influence each other's responses. The group's discussions will be facilitated in a non-directive way by a moderator. It will normally be taped and last around two hours. The moderators must have a good understanding of the objectives of the research as they will have to respond instantaneously to the dynamics of the group, shifting the focus, probing on some issues, letting others drift. The minimum number of focus groups considering any topic is generally recognized to be two, although there are no standard guidelines for this.

Group interviews are based on an interview guide. Like informal interviews they will produce a large amount of data, which can be difficult to analyse. At its most sophisticated, the analysis of these data involves consideration of words, tone, context, non-verbal interactions within the group, internal consistency, specificity of responses, etc. The groups can be difficult to assemble and they may be unpredictable.

There are several variations on the group interview. Groups can, for example, be asked to reconvene and cover a range of topics over a period of time, perhaps being involved in considering the findings from previous discussions. A more sophisticated version of group interviews, the Delphi process, involves repeated cumulative sessions with the same group, focusing on particular issues and consensus building.

Using documentary sources

There is an enormous volume of qualitative data on experiences, relationships and situations available through written sources.[12] Very often research with documentary data merges into what would more properly be thought of as history or biography. This kind of information has strengths and weaknesses not shared by other more obtrusive methods, i.e. those involving direct contact between the researcher and the researched.

Documents come in all shapes and sizes, and can be classified along a number of different dimensions, such as public/private, official/unofficial, or individual/corporate. They include coroners' reports, parish or local authority records, minutes of meetings, diaries, letters and clinical notes. Additionally, there are items that we might not normally think of as documents because of their ubiquity and obviousness: newspapers, magazines, photographs, posters and handbills. The collection and collation of documentary data present mechanical problems that are different from those involved in dealing with interviews or observations, but the methodological issues are very similar. Issues to do with reliability and validity, error, bias and so forth clearly have to be considered.

Documents are 'traces' of human thoughts and activities. They allow us to delve much more deeply into 'memory' than can be done in interviews. But the source of the document will determine whose memory is being uncovered. For example, in trying to find out more about the agendas of voluntary groups in relation to health needs, one might want to attend their meetings, look at minutes, examine their mission statements and written constitutions, in addition to interviewing individuals and initiating focus group discussions. Each of these is likely to give a different perspective on, or account of, events and processes within and between organizations.

In using any kind of documentary evidence it is important to try to ascertain who produced a particular document and what it was originally intended for. It has been suggested that there are four main criteria to be used in the assessment of documentary sources.

1 *Authenticity*: is the evidence genuine and of unquestionable origin?
2 *Credibility*: is the evidence free from error and distortion?
3 *Representativeness*: is the evidence typical of its kind and, if not, is the extent of its atypicality known?
4 *Meaning*: is the evidence clear and comprehensible?

Only if the information is good in terms of these four criteria can claims be made about the validity of the interpretations and the possibility of generalizing the findings.

RAPID APPRAISAL: QUALITATIVE ACTION RESEARCH IN HEALTH NEEDS

Individual research techniques can be brought together to develop systematic research strategies. One of these, *rapid appraisal*,[13] has a particular value to purchasing authorities as they seek to involve local people in the purchasing process. Rapid appraisal was developed with a view to understanding the needs of deprived urban communities, though it can be used in other contexts. It is based on the WHO Health for All approach and is therefore concerned to increase equity, participation and multisectoral cooperation (see Chapter 2). It is an appraisal in that it provides a qualitative picture of the health and priorities of local people. It is rapid in that the whole exercise can be done in approximately ten working days.

The primary aims of rapid appraisal are: to gain insight into a community's own perspective on priority needs; to translate these findings into managerial action; and to establish an on-going relationship between service commissioners, providers and local communities. A community is primarily defined as a social entity: in practice the focus is often on a small geographical area with an upper limit population of 12 000. The emphasis is on health needs assessment, rather than health care needs assessment. This logically leads to a multi-disciplinary and multi-agency approach.

An important characteristic of rapid appraisal is that, at least ideally, instead of separate research workers feeding results back to managers, managers themselves are the researchers. Although it is possible to undertake a rapid appraisal without direct managerial involvement in data gathering, such involvement has been shown to maximize the potential value of the exercise.

Rapid appraisal involves eight stages.

1 An initial workshop (normally two full days) to examine the scope of the method, generate the key questions for the research, determine the target population and respondents, and set out the work schedule. This should involve a multi-disciplinary, multi-agency team of managers directly involved in commissioning and providing services in the target area.
2 Fieldwork, consisting of open-ended interviews with the selected respondents.
3 A workshop (maximum half-day) for the whole team to distil the qualitative data into a list of needs as defined by the community.

4 A return to the respondents to ask them to put the list of needs into priority order.
5 Analysis (computer-assisted or manual) of the priority listings obtained by members of the interviewing teams.
6 A workshop (maximum half-day) to formulate a composite priority list.
7 An open meeting with the community to decide the first set of priorities for action, and to agree specific action plans;
8 Regular evaluation of progress, and subsequent revision of action plans.

The strategy provides an appraisal of the strength of feeling in a community through interviews with so-called key informants. This approach is based on the premise that there is not one 'truth' about a community's needs. Rather, understanding is built up through a variety of perspectives. Thus, information is collected from different categories of knowledgeable people:

● people who work as professionals in the community, e.g. teachers, health visitors, policemen, etc.;
● elected and self-elected leaders' insights, such as councillors, chairs of self-help groups, etc.;
● people who occupy a central position in the community because of their location or particular function, e.g. the corner shop owner, lollipop person, turf accountant.

It is important, in building up a valid picture, to scrutinize the choice of informants carefully. An attempt should be made to cover all (or most) perspectives and to include contrasting views. A 'snowball' approach to constructing the sample of key informants is useful.

The main research work will be carried out by the managers of the various organizations. The ideal configuration for a team would include participation from the health sector (DHA, FHSA, GP fund-holders, provider units), social services, housing, education, environmental health and other local authority departments when relevant.

The qualitative information generated through interviews with local informants should be complemented with information of a more quantitative kind drawn from various different sources, including the census, NHS activity data, existing survey data on health status, health related behaviour, etc. Together these sources of information should feed into the final preparation of a draft action plan, which will form the basis of discussions with the local community.

The final product from a rapid appraisal is a clear action plan (or plans) for joint working between a community and statutory and voluntary organizations. This will be based on an understanding of priority needs between local people and service representatives. Progress should be monitored jointly by assessing whether the objectives of the various plans have been achieved. Therefore, plans have to be defined as realistic, with participation by all parties, and achievable within a relatively short time frame, such as six months. Regular meetings will be necessary to monitor implementation and progress.

The findings of a rapid appraisal provide a snapshot in time, and not necessarily a stable picture over time. As part of the evaluation of the planned, joint action between the community and the managers of services, a new rapid appraisal can be undertaken. This will also refocus the agenda, and help to stimulate a continuing programme of work.

Success in rapid appraisal requires a willingness to work across disciplines and organizations. This means that good listening is a fundamental requirement. Managers also have to be willing to engage in discussions with communities about different perceptions of priorities. This can sometimes be uncomfortable. For example, in one of the communities where rapid appraisal was used, people said they did not feel that immunization and vaccination should be continued. However, listening to local people does not mean that one has to do exactly what they want. The central objective is to establish a dialogue about the priorities of both sides, out of which can come compromise and agreed joint action.

Rapid appraisal also requires some formal skills. For example, those involved need some understanding of open-ended interviewing and how to analyse qualitative data. Computer skills are also useful, but not essential. The primary strength of rapid appraisal is that it provides insight into a community's experience and people's perceptions of their needs. Ultimately, these are the factors that will determine whether people are actively involved in issues affecting their health.

Rapid appraisal can also mobilize managers from different sectors and organizations. However, it has to be acknowledged that senior managers tend to move frequently. Middle managers may be able to develop more stable relationships with a community but they tend to have less decision-making power. Their involvement means that the action-oriented aspects of rapid appraisal may not move as rapidly as they should. The choice of manager and researchers therefore has to be done carefully.

Rapid appraisal is a research strategy that also directly addresses the NHS remit of involving local people in purchasing: it asks people to formulate their needs and priorities and then engages them in a debate about the commissioning of services. Through this process they will be in a better position to evaluate both service content (i.e. are resources allocated in such a way that it addresses their need?) and service form (i.e. are services delivered in a user-friendly manner?).

CONCLUSION

In this chapter we have tried to show what is required of health needs assessment once a sociological view of need is taken seriously. To simplify this view considerably, it involves listening to and taking seriously what local people have to say about their needs. The philosophers and social policy experts mentioned at the beginning of this chapter articulate concerns about the relations between individuals, civil society and the state. Although these writings may seem somewhat distant from the interests, agendas and timetables of purchasers in hard-pressed health authorities, they can help to inform our approaches to understanding what people need. Individuals experience needs in situations that may facilitate or constrain the expression of them.

Divisions in society between lay and professional people are undergoing profound changes. Indeed, one historian has gone so far as to raise the prospect of the end of professional society. Whatever one makes of the shifting ground of consumer and professional relationships, it is certainly clear that health needs in the twenty-first century are going to require something other than the imperious judgements of professionals passed down to clients or patients like tablets of stone. The realities of intersectoral collaboration and public participation are fraught with difficulties, but unless professionals begin to look at ways of addressing these issues effectively within the needs assessment process the opportunities of the current situation will be lost. We have suggested in this chapter an approach to research methods that will help in this endeavour. If the assessment of need is approached from this perspective then the opportunities for health gain through the commissioning of services to meet need will be considerably enhanced.

REFERENCES

1 Plant, R., Lesser, A. H. and Taylor-Gooby, P. (1981) *Political Philosophy and Social Welfare*. London: Routledge.
2 Ignatieff, M. (1984) *The Needs of Strangers*. London: Chatto and Windus.
3 Bradhaw, J. (1992) The conceptualisation and measurement of need: a social policy perspective. Paper delivered to the Economic and Social Research Council seminar on Social Research and Needs Assessment, Salford Royal Hospital, Salford, January.
4 Williams, G. (1991) Disablement and the ideological crisis in health care. *Social Science and Medicine*, **32**, 517–24.
5 Allsop, J. (1984) *Health Policy and the National Health Service*. Harlow: Longman.
6 There are a number of general guides to qualitative research, e.g. Walker, R. (ed.) (1985) *Applied Qualitative Research*. Aldershot: Gower. Another practical guide is Riley, J. (1990) *Getting the Most from Your Data: a Handbook of Practical Ideas on How to Analyse Qualitative Data*. Bristol: Technical and Educational Services Ltd. For a more realistic description of research processes see Bell, C. and Newby, H. (eds) (1977) *Doing Sociological Research*. London: George Allen and Unwin.
7 Last, J. M. (1988) *A Dictionary of Epidemiology*. Oxford: Oxford University Press.
8 A good example is McKeganey, N., Barnard, M. and Bloor, M. (1990) A comparison of HIV related risk behaviour and risk reduction between female

streetworking prostitutes and male rent boys in Glasgow. *Sociology of Health and Illness*, **12**, 274–92.

9 McCall, G. and Simmons, J. (eds) (1969) *Issues in Participant Observation: a Text and Reader*. Reading, MA: Addison-Wesley.

10 McCracken, G. (1988) *The Long Interview*. London: Sage.

11 Kreuger, R. A. (1988) *Focus Groups: A Practical Guide for Applied Research*. London: Sage.

12 Scott, J. (1990) *A Matter of Record: Documentary Sources in Social Research*. Cambridge: Polity Press.

13 The key texts are: Annett, H. and Rifkin, S. (1988) *Improving Urban Health*. Geneva: World Health Organization; Ong, B. N. and Humphris, G. (1990) Partners in need. *Health Service Journal*, 5 July, 1002–3; Ong, B. N., Humphris, G., Annett, H. and Rifkin, S. (1991) Rapid appraisal in an urban setting: an example from the developed world. *Social Science in Medicine*, **32**, 909–15.

5 / THE LIFE CYCLE FRAMEWORK – ITS RATIONALE, STRUCTURE AND USE

This chapter explains the rationale, structure and use of the life cycle framework. The framework itself is presented in the following nine chapters and the reader should find it helpful to refer to those chapters during this exposition.

THE NATURE OF FRAMEWORKS

It should be clear from Chapters 2 and 3 that the tasks associated with health needs assessment are not easy and that they call upon a variety of skills. In approaching tasks of this complexity it is tempting to begin by assembling diverse sources of information about the population under scrutiny. However, we believe this course of action to be unproductive. The reasons why are clearly stated in the following quotations from letters from Charles Darwin to contemporaries:

> About thirty years ago there was much talk that geologists ought only to observe and not theorize; and I well remember someone saying that at this rate a man might as well go into a gravel-pit and count the pebbles and describe the colours. How odd it is that any-one should not see that all observation must be for or against some view if it is to be of any service.

I have an old belief that a good observer really means a good theorist.

These quotations were cited by Medawar[1] in support of his contention that, despite what some practising scientists might claim, scientific endeavour proceeds through observation directed by prior hypotheses rather than through observation alone. We, of course, are not here concerned with pure scientific enquiry. However, we do assert that the assessment of health needs includes a series of activities that require the same clarity of thought and no less rigour in its engagement. Thus, we must reject haphazard ramblings through the 'gravel pit' and seek only information whose purpose is understood in advance.

In this context there are two requirements. The first is detailed policies to direct purchasing for health gain and the sub-task of health needs assessment; this will be discussed further in Chapter 15. The second is a framework to make the steps involved in health needs assessment coherent. A brief discussion of the general nature of frameworks will help to set our biological life cycle framework in context.

A framework may merely be a structure that helps to divide complicated concepts and/or tasks into smaller ones. If a framework is to be something more than an arbitrary division then there should be a clear logical relationship between its components. Nevertheless, a logical framework, of which the life cycle framework is an example, is not the same as a theoretical framework (or, more simply, a theory). The distinction is important because the two kinds of framework arouse different kinds of expectations.

The former is a tool to assist in practical tasks. Its justification is pragmatic: it should be robust in the sense that it will not need to be abandoned as knowledge or fashions (e.g. theories and ideologies) change. The latter is an encapsulation of knowledge and understanding; it might describe, or preferably predict, events and behaviours within its domain and thus be of practical use. If it is truly a scientific theory it is capable of refutation through the comparison of predictions with observations. There is no contender for a universal theory of health to direct health needs assessment.

The life cycle framework is pragmatic but it is not wholly atheoretical; it is something of a hybrid between the two kinds of framework. It will become clear that it draws on well established biological and epidemiological concepts and happily incorporates a variety of theories (and views) about various biological and non-biological influences on health and health needs. But it is not wholly dependent on the 'truth' of these and is capable of absorbing new insights. At its simplest the framework is merely descriptive: it is an *aide-mémoire* of health needs and information sources. However, as will be shown, it can guide health needs assessment and also has the potential to become a powerful planning tool.

THE LIFE CYCLE FRAMEWORK, THE MEDICAL MODEL
OF DISEASE AND BEYOND

The life cycle framework starts from what is often referred to as the medical model of disease and illness. It recognizes explicitly that illness and the potential for illness are always at least partially explicable in biological terms. At the most fundamental level it is well known that the potential for health or illness is largely determined by the 'hand' of genes one received from one's parents. That being so, a proportion of the variation in health and disease experiences observed in the population is attributable to this source. However, except in a few instances we are as yet unable to assess an individual's potential health needs through genetic analysis.

At the next level it is recognized that how the 'hand' of genes is played depends upon the passage of time. We each pass through a biological life cycle starting at infancy and ending at death (potentially) in old age. There are well recognized stages to the life cycle, such as suckling, puberty, the major reproductive period and senescence. People reach the varying stages at roughly the same chronological ages. It would seem that in humans as in other animals the 'hand' of genes defines a clock.

Biology, however, is not the only cause of differences in life experience at different ages. The social structure of society also has its effect. Some influences are socially rather than biologically determined, such as adolescence or adulthood. Life experiences are a combination of both social and biological effects (e.g. the experience of old age). Thus the social and economic arrangements of mankind introduce a host of complicating factors and these are associated with a variety of life-styles that interact, in ill-understood ways, with our various genetic 'hands of cards'.

The various stages in the biological and social life cycle are associated with particular opportunities to promote health and with particular risks of ill-health. For instance, a variety of infectious diseases affect mainly the very young; the cancers and most other chronic diseases predominantly affect the middle-aged and elderly. Any division of the biological and social life cycle into discrete age groups will be arbitrary (and for some individuals inappropriate). We selected nine life cycle stages (age groups). These are displayed in Table 5.1. For each life cycle stage some key health/illness issues are illustrated. Each of Chapters 6 to 14 refers to one such stage.

Genetic, other biological and social considerations are alone insufficient to explain the observed patterns of health and ill-health in human populations. The natural environment influences how a 'hand' of genes is played. In some circumstances one 'hand' might be particularly advantageous whereas in other circumstances a different 'hand' would be more useful. Nature has a habit of playing joker cards, which can suddenly change the odds in the game. These occurrences are hard to document

Table 5.1   Life cycle age groups

Age group	Some key health/illness issues
Late pregnancy to one week after birth	quality of pregnancy, delivery and early life, mother's health
One week to one year	quality of the immediate external environment, quality of the home environment, immunization, developmental surveillance, family influences
One to four years	immunization, home accidents, the immediate external environment, special needs groups, family influences
Five to 14 years	accidents outside the home, malignancies, formal education and preparation for a healthy life-style, special needs groups, peer group influences
15 to 24 years	preparation for healthy, independent adult life, accidents, in particular road traffic accidents, violence, self-inflicted injury, risky behaviour, e.g. alcohol and drug use, sexual activity, sexually transmitted disease including HIV, child-bearing, family planning, homelessness, stress, peer group pressures
25 to 44 years	child-bearing, child-rearing, accidents, malignancies, unhealthy life-style, special needs, work-related illness, mental health, health promotion, development of autonomy, stress
45 to 64 years	coronary heart disease, stroke, malignancies, chronic illness, work related illness, respiratory disease, screening, e.g. for breast cancer and CHD risk factors, mental health, preparation for old age
65 to 74 years	all major causes of acute and chronic illness, disability (particularly impairment of mobility and sensation), dementia and depression, maintenance of function and independence, social isolation
75 years and over	multiple morbidity, dementia and depression, maintenance of function and independence, social isolation, quality of housing

except in a few cases. One such is sickle cell anaemia. In this case the presence of one abnormal gene in a pair confers an advantage to individuals if they are living in an area where malaria is very common but a clear disadvantage if the individuals are not living in such an area.

Mankind has to cope not only with the changes of the natural environment but also with those of our artificial environment. This has brought about many opportunities and risks that had no part in fashioning, through evolution, the sets of genes present today. For instance, we are exposed to physical and chemical influences (e.g. pollution) unknown in mankind's distant past.

Clearly, any attempt to assess health needs that relied solely upon a narrow medical model would be ignoring influences which could be as great, or even greater, than the biological factors discussed above. Indeed, the most fundamental biological factor, genetic make-up, is, at our present state of knowledge, unalterable. Thus, pragmatically, we must concentrate on those things that can be influenced. The potential for influence ranges from advice, or services, for individuals, through traditional public health measures that protect populations, to restructuring society.

MODIFIERS TO HEALTH EXPERIENCE

The life cycle framework explicitly acknowledges these wider influences on health status and health needs through the concept of modifiers. These are classified under four headings:

- socio-economic;
- environmental;
- ethnic (includes both racial effects and generalized cultural influences dependent on ethnic origin and background);
- cultural (includes potential local cultural influences).

Each chapter on a life cycle stage contains a general account of influences on health and existing health resources appropriate to that stage. The modifiers are introduced to remind the reader of known associations between specified factors and susceptibility to ill-health, and the need for service provision or access to service provision in sub-groups of the population. This information should be used to tune the assessment of health need in defined populations.

For instance, in Chapter 6 there is a brief discussion of the strong statistical association between social class and perinatal mortality; environmental hazards (e.g. radiation) to the fetus are mentioned; under the heading of ethnic modifiers the increased perinatal mortality of babies born to women from the New Commonwealth is discussed; the section on cultural modifiers mentions the raised perinatal mortality of births outside marriage.

SECULAR AND BIOLOGICAL CHRONOLOGIES

The structure of the life cycle framework, with its primary division into life cycle stages, sits easily with the notion of cohort analysis introduced in Chapter 3. Each life cycle stage corresponds to an aggregation of birth cohorts. Thus the childhood stage (5–14 years) encompasses in 1993 the set of birth cohorts born between 1979 and 1988.

When looking at populations through the life cycle framework it should be borne in mind that at any point in time one is examining a static picture of a dynamic population process. The lifetime influences on health of the aggregate 5–14 year cohorts will have been very different by the time their survivors reach their sixties than those of people currently in their sixties. For instance, as a result of the clean air legislation, reduction of air pollution in work-places and falls in the prevalence of cigarette smoking, chronic lung disease will become much less common in the middle-aged and elderly.

The life cycle framework in its present form makes little explicit mention of cohort and period effects (see Chapter 3) but does, by definition, make great use of age effects.

SUMMARY OF THE STRUCTURE OF THE LIFE CYCLE FRAMEWORK

Each of Chapters 6 to 14 has the same basic structure, as shown below.

1 *Influences on health*   A general account of the main influences on health in that life cycle stage, followed by lists of the leading causes of mortality (deaths) and morbidity (ill-health).
2 *Sources of information on health*   A list of the readily available information and its sources. The section is divided into demography (matters pertaining to population structure), mortality and morbidity.
3 *Modifiers to health experience*   This section summarizes the major known socio-economic, environmental, ethnic and cultural modifiers of health experience. Sources of information about each modifier are listed.
4 *Health resources*   Health resources available to improve the health experience of the life cycle stage are listed. These are subdivided into those within the individual, the family, the community and formal health services. The last are divided into health care (health promotion, primary care and secondary care), local authority, private sector and voluntary sector.
5 *Modifiers to the use of services*   This section examines how people's use of services is influenced by socio-economic, environmental, ethnic and cultural factors.
6 *Service options*   This section is intended to stimulate discussion about ways of improving existing services and consideration of new service

options. It focuses particularly on primary care because at a population level this is a vital health resource which is often overlooked in the process of health needs assessment.

USING THE LIFE CYCLE FRAMEWORK

At the simplest level the life cycle framework may be used as a handy reference and *aide-mémoire* for looking at the three tasks of assessing the health needs of defined populations. It highlights the health issues to consider at each life cycle stage; it summarizes the currently available routine information sources; and it outlines service options to meet needs. The user, within the context of the policy directives within which he or she is working, may rapidly decide how to structure the particular task and put to best use the information presented in the framework. Moreover, the framework helps to direct attention to areas where knowledge is sparse and the user may decide to supplement routine information sources by *ad hoc* enquiry, including research. Furthermore, the framework forms a basis for users to construct and publish their own population profiles. As local knowledge grows and information sources develop the user may easily slot these into the overall framework.

In the following we describe in more detail how the lifecycle framework may be used. There are four steps.

STEP 1 is to identify pertinent life cycle stages. The choice of these will be determined by the issues at hand, in particular the priorities of the organization as a whole. Sometimes it will be clear at the outset that only particular stages need to be examined. For instance, if it has been decided to turn attention to the immediate needs of the elderly then attention may be restricted to the final two life cycle stages. If the aim is to seek measures to promote good health and minimize dependency by the elderly then attention might be directed towards the seventh (middle-age) and eighth (early old age) life cycle stages.

On other occasions attention may initially be focused on a particular disease (e.g. diabetes) or problem (e.g. health of the homeless) rather than life cycle stages *per se*. In these instances it should be recognized that the health status, the nature and the quantity of needs, and the means of addressing them usually differ according to life cycle stage. Thus an analysis by life cycle stage is helpful in reducing a heterogeneous collection of issues into more homogeneous and manageable ones. This way of using the life cycle framework will be explored again below.

STEP 2 is, as far as is practicable, to quantify the extent of the health needs and problems within each appropriate life cycle stage. The matter of quantification is central to using health needs assessment in NHS purchasing. We shall discuss this in Chapter 15 but for the present five points need to be made.

1   Some aspects of health status and health resources are more easy to quantify than others. There is a danger that what can be quantified will take precedence over what cannot, i.e. there may be a tendency to believe that problems to which numbers cannot be attached are unimportant. On the one hand a growth and improvement of routine health service information systems consequent upon the NHS purchaser function is to be welcomed. On the other hand those who care about the health of the whole community should be wary of seeing the extent of the world as being that which is within the information technology systems.

2   Quantification is not an all or nothing activity. It has degrees. For some issues it may be possible to attach precise numbers, for many estimates, for some educated guesses, and for some the best that can be achieved may be to attach a rank order with respect to other issues.

3   Merely identifying a need or problem gives a lower bound to the extent of the problem, i.e. the problem does exist and there are at least so many known instances. A mere prose description of the nature of some problems or needs is a useful starting contribution to health needs assessment.

4   It is possible to plan services and distribute resources in the absence of precise knowledge of the extent of the problems being met. The NHS has done this for years. The mere identification of important needs as yet not met, but capable of being met, is itself an advance.

5   In utopia health needs assessment would lead to the quantification of all needs, which potentially could be met. However, in our world the bottom line, where the numbers must add up correctly, is the division of the financial resource available for meeting needs.

Attempts at quantification will call upon many existing information sources. In addition, when the problems of interest have been determined in advance, thinking is not constrained by what information happens to exist; new sources of information, either routine or *ad hoc*, may be called for.

STEP 3 is to apply health modifiers to each life cycle stage. The effects of some health modifiers might be known with some precision. Generally, however, applying the modifiers will entail qualitative information sources, research and judgements. Awareness of the modifiers is useful for directing attention to sub-groups of each life cycle stage who may have particular problems or needs. In so far as the overall health status and health needs profiles are concerned some modifiers assist in quantifying the degree of the severity or urgency of health problems.

STEP 4 is to relate the health status profile produced by steps 1, 2 and 3 to health resources, which will include both policies and services.

Health needs assessment is the process by which a health status profile of a community is related to the health resources available to that community in order to achieve a desired outcome. The health resources available are not restricted to those provided by the NHS but include those provided by other sectors, voluntary groups and the community itself, both families and individuals. Use of the life cycle framework highlights the role of the non-NHS providers of services and clarifies the need for a multi-sectoral approach, which involves the community. It also helps to clarify the areas where the NHS – both primary and secondary levels – can begin to address the health needs of a community through re-distribution of these resources through the purchasing process.

As an example of the foregoing, consider the purchasing of services for mothers with young children. From the first step of the exercise the typical problems and needs of these women and their children will have been identified; initially attention is likely to be concentrated on the fifth and sixth life cycle stages for females. The second step will discover the current number of mothers with young children living within the administrative boundaries of, say, a family health service authority. Furthermore, the likely numbers of people with or about to develop various problems or needs will be quantified.

At the third step the following issues might be considered: the spatial distribution and concentrations of mothers with young children within the FHSA area and how this distribution relates to the provision of GP and health authority community services. Perhaps particular practices should by virtue of their position be specially funded and encouraged to care for, say, their more than average number of mothers with young children. How does the present distribution relate to the socio-economic status of these people? This relates partly to how the prevalence of various problems varies among socio-economic groups and partly to the differing abilities of these groups to access and make good use of the type of services on offer. Thus, city FHSAs may need to weight resources towards more disadvantaged social groups. This issue also has to be examined spatially. Inner-city practices may require greater per capita patient funding (including provision of health visitors etc.) than suburban practices. People's ethnic background can modify their experience of ill-health as well as affecting their likelihood of using services. The ethnic background of the group under examination needs to be explored and information on religion, language, literacy rates and culture obtained. Aside from ethnicity there may be local cultural values that influence health-related behaviours or health service usage, and these factors should be identified as part of health needs assessment. This will involve both qualitative research and the involvement of the local community. General environmental considerations include the presence of known environmental hazards or poor environmental conditions, such as industrial works or the presence of poor housing stock.

At the fourth step packages of health resources, from any sector, will be sought to meet the identified needs of mothers with young children. These will be costed and put alongside the packages of health resources identified for other needs groups (e.g. the elderly) before the final decision is taken on how the total available resources for health will be spent on the community's behalf.

The life cycle approach does not prevent purchasers or planners from looking at groups defined in other ways. Indeed, it gives a structured approach to these too. Consider the example of the homeless mentioned above. These constitute a group of people not initially defined by biological life cycle. Nevertheless, the homeless, once identified as a group of particular interest, can be viewed in life cycle terms. Questions such as the following emerge. How many homeless are there? How many are young and single and what particular risks are they prone to? How many are single in middle and late life and what problems are they prone to? How many homeless families are there? How many have young children? How are the various categories of homeless distributed spatially? What kind of services do they require? Are services provided in the right places to meet the needs of the homeless? Should specific services be created or existing ones tailored to their needs? Are there any ethnic or cultural modifiers that need to be taken into account?

Similarly, the framework is applicable to disease based groups. For instance, the needs of eight year old diabetics are entirely different from those of 80 year old diabetics. Moreover, they differ between a white middle-class diabetic and an Asian diabetic from a less affluent area.

This account of how the life cycle framework might be used in practice is not intended to be prescriptive. The framework will have served a useful purpose even if it is only used in an informal manner to guide initial thinking about an assessment task. It is left to the user to explore its potential and determine the best way of employing it.

Chapters 6 to 14 present the framework in detail. Chapter 15 puts the process of assessment of health need into the wider context of purchasing for health gain.

REFERENCE

1 Medawar, P. B. (1970) *Induction and Intuition in Scientific Thought*. London: Methuen.

6 / LIFE STAGE: FROM LATE PREGNANCY TO ONE WEEK AFTER BIRTH

1 INFLUENCES ON HEALTH

The fetus and very young infant are very sensitive to adverse environmental influences. Before birth the mother provides the environment for the baby and therefore her health is of prime importance to the baby's health and survival. In relation to the rest of the person's life experience birth is a risky time for survival. This is both because birth itself is a traumatic process and because birth requires an adaptation from the intrauterine environment to the extrauterine. This can be difficult, particularly for an already compromised fetus.

Mortality

The cause of death in babies up to one week old is not routinely available. However, it has been estimated that about 40 per cent of deaths occurring under one year can be accounted for by the perinatal period (time around birth). Deaths can be attributed to three major causes:

1 Low birth weight or prematurity.
2 Congenital abnormalities: there are many of these but the most usual are congenital heart disease and spina bifida with hydrocephalus.
3 Birth injury.

Morbidity

If not fatal, all of the above can cause both limiting and long-standing illness and disability. In addition, other diseases that are unlikely to cause death are likely to make very young babies unwell. As the vast majority of babies are born in hospital in the UK we can use hospital diagnoses to give an indication of the extent and nature of the likely morbidity patterns.

Unfortunately, hospital diagnoses in this age group are somewhat vague. The most common diagnoses in babies under one week old in the North Western Region of England are:

1 Neonatal jaundice.
2 Prematurity.
3 Illness associated with a breech delivery (born feet first).
4 Illness associated with a caesarian section.
5 Illness associated with forceps delivery.
6 Fetal distress.

2 SOURCES OF INFORMATION ON HEALTH

The following are routinely available for each district health authority from the public health medicine department.

2.1 Demography

Number of live births.
Number of premature births.
Number of stillbirths, i.e. those fetuses born after 28 weeks gestation who show no sign of life at birth.
Births by birth weight for both live births and stillbirths.

All the above are available by the age of the mother.

2.2 Mortality

The *perinatal mortality rate* (PNMR) is the number of stillbirths plus the number of babies who die in the first week after birth as a proportion of all live births and stillbirths. The PNMR is also available for smaller areas than districts but great care must be taken in comparing small area rates as these are based on small numbers of deaths (see Chapter 3). To monitor trends a more reliable indicator is three-year moving averages.

Information on deaths from congenital abnormalities is available by type of congenital abnormality and by district health authority.

2.3 Morbidity

Routine hospital data include the Körner Episode System (KES), which can give diagnoses, length of stay and whether the hospital stay ended in death or discharge.

Other sources of data on this age group include antenatal records, health visitor records and GP records. To utilize these sources would require special surveys.

Information on congenital abnormalities picked up in this age group is available.

3 MODIFIERS TO HEALTH EXPERIENCE

3.1 Socio-economic

Perinatal mortality is strongly associated with social class; the PNMR is least for the highest social classes (social classes I and II) and progressively increases to be greatest among the unskilled (social class V). This probably relates to lower disposable income contributing to the general poorer health, and consequent smaller stature, of less well-off mothers; other important contributing factors include an increased prevalence of smoking and less opportunity to rest. All these lead to an increased risk of a low birth-weight baby. Overcrowding and damp housing increase the risk of infections in the mother, some of which can damage the fetus. Research has shown that working-class women have less free time to rest during pregnancy and less flexibility in their daily routines.

Sources of information
Social class, unemployment rates, number receiving housing benefit, car ownership, level of basic amenities and housing tenure type can all indicate levels of social deprivation. Composite scores include the Jarman (see Glossary) and Townsend, both of which are available at ward level; the former will also be available at practice level.

3.2 Environmental

Environmental hazards to the fetus include exposure to known teratogens (substances known to be capable of damaging the fetus), e.g. radiation.

Poor diet of the mother, particularly low vitamin intake, may increase the likelihood of spina bifida and other similar congenital defects.

Sources of information
Local knowledge of possible sources of environmental hazards and levels of radiation may be available from the environmental health department of the local authority. Assessment of the availability of fresh fruit and vegetables, particularly among the most socially deprived groups, will require a special survey. Local knowledge may give some idea, however.

3.3   Ethnic

There is an increased PNMR among babies born to women from the New Commonwealth and Pakistan. This is likely to be greater than that accounted for by social class alone. Research suggests that the following are contributing factors:

- low birth weight;
- poor antenatal attendance;
- anaemia;
- large number of pregnancies and births;
- small stature;
- consanguinity (marriage between close relatives, e.g. cousins).

There is some evidence that the offspring of Afro-Caribbean women also have a higher perinatal mortality rate. Most of this is probably accounted for by higher levels of social deprivation. However, an increased risk of hypertension (high blood pressure) during pregnancy may contribute.

Sources of information
Census data provide a breakdown of the place of birth of the head of household. These are routinely available at district level and can be broken down to electoral ward level. Unfortunately this does not give information on women born in this country who would still be considered as part of an ethnic minority group. The 1991 census should provide more useful information as it asked a question on perceived ethnic group membership.

Other sources of information on the ethnic composition of your local population include local community group leaders and the Community Relations Council. They can provide information on country of origin, language and religious background of ethnic minority groups. This type of information is essential for the more effective understanding of the problems and needs of diverse ethnic groups.

3.4 *Cultural*

(a) Birth outside marriage

Babies born outside marriage (previously labelled illegitimate births) show a higher PNMR, although this is decreasing. The effect is probably almost totally brought about through social class differences. As births outside marriage becomes more usual among middle-class families and in families where the relationship between the mother and father is a stable one this effect is likely to decrease.

Sources of information
The proportion of births outside marriage is routinely collected and available to health authorities and local authorities.

(b) Age of mother

Very young mothers are likely to have low birth-weight babies. The risk of certain congenital abnormalities, e.g. Down's syndrome, increases with the age of the mother.

Sources of information
Births tabulated by age are available at district health authority level. Special analysis of the original data is needed if these tables are required on a small area basis for use in primary care.

4 HEALTH RESOURCES

Health resources available to this group include:

Within the individual
At this age the only health resources within the individual will result from genetic make-up and therefore are not easily altered.

Within the family
- Family income;
- education of mother;
- health of mother;
- family support;
- communication within the family.

Within the community
- Community support networks;
- community spirit;
- neighbourliness;
- child-minders;

- babysitting circles;
- church and other community religious groups;
- local health-related pressure groups;
- facilities for mothers with babies.

Health service
Health education/promotion:
- community development;
- patient-held records/cooperation card;
- information on smoking, diet and exercise in pregnancy, with support to change behaviour;
- parenthood education in schools.

Primary care:
- antenatal clinics;
- antenatal classes;
- pre-conceptual care;
- community midwives;
- health visitors;
- home delivery service;
- GP obstetric unit;

Secondary care:
- antenatal clinics;
- antenatal classes;
- obstetric services;
- obstetric flying squad;
- special care baby unit.

Local authority
Social services department:
- family worker scheme.

Housing department:
- policy for homeless pregnant women;
- provision of cheap, high quality public sector housing.

Private sector
- Availability of cheap, wholesome food;
- availability of transport systems to health care services;
- provision of recreation facilities;
- provision of activities that foster social support;
- availability of cheap, high quality housing for rent.

Voluntary sector
- Parenthood classes;
- National Childbirth Trust classes and information.

5   MODIFIERS TO USE OF SERVICES

5.1   Socio-economic

How far they have to travel to services is an important issue for women from working-class areas. This is because they are less likely to have access to a car and will have less income for bus fares. They may also have to travel on public transport with their other young children with them as they are less able to pay for childcare while attending clinics etc. All this makes attending a clinic for working-class women more of a burden than for most other women. Crèches in health service facilities may encourage women with small children to attend.

Sources of information
Travel times to major hospitals from electoral wards are routinely available.

5.2   Environmental

The environment for the fetus is the mother's womb. The mother's environment can influence intrauterine environment, e.g. through exposure to radiation and other teratogens in the atmosphere. Infectious diseases in the air, water supply or foodstuffs can in some cases cause illness, disability or death in the fetus or newborn baby, e.g. listeriosis in soft cheeses and pâté, rubella, toxoplasmosis, cytomegalovirus.

Sources of information
The environmental health department may have some information on known environmental hazards.

5.3   Ethnic

For pregnant women whose first language is not English there is a need for health education material in other languages, interpreters at antenatal classes and/or midwives and health visitors who speak other languages. In areas where there is a large number of women from the Asian subcontinent the availability of women doctors is crucial. (It is desirable for all women to have the choice of seeing a woman doctor during pregnancy.)

Sources of information
Local surveys of antenatal clinics in primary and secondary care will be required.

5.4   Cultural

The local culture, regardless of income differences, may affect perceptions of the usefulness of attending clinics and classes. It will certainly
affect the norm regarding unhealthy behaviours during pregnancy and
is known to influence the likelihood of the baby being breast fed.

Sources of information
Anthropological and sociological studies or consumer satisfaction studies
may highlight the issues. Advice on how to carry out these can be
obtained from many sources, including your public health medicine
department.

6   SERVICE OPTIONS IN PRIMARY CARE

6.1   Pre-conceptual care

This aims to provide advice to couples who are considering trying to
conceive. It aims to promote the health of the fetus by encouraging the
woman to prepare for pregnancy. It could include advice on stopping
smoking and reducing alcohol consumption, advice on a diet rich in
fresh fruit and vegetables, and genetic counselling if appropriate. If this
service is provided it will need to be appropriate to the population it
wishes to serve, e.g. with interpreters and health education materials in
other languages if necessary.

6.2   Antenatal clinics

These should offer:
- ready access to a woman doctor;
- a crèche;
- an interpreter if required;
- appropriate health education material;
- evening clinics for working mothers;
- special classes for very young mothers if appropriate;
- welfare rights information;

6.3   Obstetric care

There are a range of options for involvement of the primary care services
in obstetric care in the NHS. These include the following:

(a)   Shared obstetric care

Most women plan to have their babies in hospital and they sign on with
an obstetrician. If no abnormality is found at booking and the GP is

willing then the woman will generally be accepted for shared care. In this the birth occurs in hospital but the hospital and the GP share the antenatal care. Usually the woman visits each of them alternately during her pregnancy.

(b)   A GP obstetric unit

In this circumstance the woman receives antenatal care solely from her GP, who is also responsible with the community midwife for the birth. However, the birth takes place in a special unit in the maternity hospital and other specialist staff and equipment are available in an emergency.

(c)   Domino (domiciliary in and out) unit

In this scheme the woman is booked in with a consultant at the hospital but once she has been accepted on to the scheme all her antenatal care is provided by the GP and a community midwife. Once in labour the woman is visited at home by the community midwife but is transferred to the domino unit before delivery. The community midwife delivers the baby but if there are any problems the woman's care is taken over by the consultant with whom she is booked.

(d)   Home delivery

In this situation the GP accepts responsibility for full antenatal care and care during delivery, with an agreement that the delivery will take place in the woman's own home. Should an emergency occur the woman is transported to the maternity hospital.

6.4   Care for special groups

One option is the employment of link workers in areas where many women are from an ethnic minority background. Link workers can liaise with service providers and advise on the appropriateness of services. They can also work with women from ethnic minority backgrounds to explain the reasons for and workings of antenatal and obstetric services.

7 / LIFE STAGE: FROM ONE WEEK TO ONE YEAR

1 INFLUENCES ON HEALTH

Congenital abnormalities and perinatal influences still have a large bearing on both survival and level of ill-health in this stage but the external environment is becoming increasingly more important, particularly after the first month of life. After this time respiratory infections and accidents take a significant toll on life. An ill-defined condition known as *sudden infant death syndrome* or 'cot death' is the commonest cause of death nationally in this age group.

Mortality

Nationally the major causes of mortality in this group are:

1 Sudden infant death syndrome (SIDS).
2 Congenital abnormalities, in particular congenital heart disease and spina bifida.
3 Diseases of the respiratory system.
4 Diseases of the nervous system.
5 Fetal malnutrition or immaturity.

6 Accidents.
7 Birth asphyxia (lack of oxygen at birth).

These causes account for 70 per cent of deaths in this age group.

Morbidity

Routine information is hard to come by in this age group.

(a) Hospital admissions

The major causes of hospital admission in this age group in the North Western Region of England are:

- respiratory diseases, mainly infections;
- diarrhoea;
- vomiting;
- convulsions;
- inguinal hernia repair.

These diagnoses accounted for only 40 per cent of admission episodes, however. It must be remembered that hospital admissions are as much a reflection of bed availability, referral rates and admission policies as an indicator of need.

(b) GP consultations

There is little information on GP consultations in this age group.

(c) Other causes of ill health in this group

Accidents These occur predominantly within the home.

Infectious diseases These are an important cause of ill-health in the infant. The actual morbidity caused by infections in this age group is usually minor, with few long-term consequences. More importantly, however, some infectious diseases are a potential cause of serious morbidity and even death. Many of these, which used to be common in this age group, are very rare now (e.g. diphtheria, polio and tetanus). However, they remain a serious threat if the immunization rates fall. Others, although rarely life-threatening, carry a small risk of serious consequences as well as causing much pain and suffering (e.g. whooping cough, measles and mumps).

All the infections mentioned above are preventable by immunization. Infections common in this age group that are not preventable by vaccination are respiratory infections, meningitis and those which cause gastroenteritis.

Many childhood infections are notifiable diseases and as such every medical practitioner is legally obliged to notify the environmental health department of the local authority of any cases. Unfortunately most cases are not reported, but the system is useful for assessing trends and predicting epidemics.

The vaccination and immunization programme is a national programme in which children are called at two, three and four months for diphtheria, polio and pertussis (whooping cough) vaccination and in the second year of life for vaccination against measles, mumps and rubella (MMR). A pre-school booster is given for diphtheria, tetanus and polio. Uptake ratios for the vaccinations are assumed to be an inverse measure of the prevalence of the diseases in the community.

Congenital abnormalities These are a rare but important cause of ill-health and disability in this age group, as children with congenital abnormalities often have heavy health service needs. They cannot always be identified in the first year of life. The commonest congenital malformations are congenital heart disease, spina bifida and Down's syndrome. The level of disability varies widely within each abnormality category and therefore it is important in planning terms to know the level of disability as well as the prevalence of the abnormality.

2 SOURCES OF INFORMATION ON HEALTH

2.1 Demography

The number and area of residence of children in this age group are routinely available.

2.2 Mortality

The *infant mortality rate* is the number of deaths in the first year of life as a proportion of all live births. It is routinely available at district level and can be worked out for smaller areas, but the small numbers involved make this less useful. It has three components:

- deaths in the first week of life, which were dealt with in Chapter 6;
- deaths in the first month of life (neonatal mortality rate), which follow a similar pattern, with perinatal influences and congenital abnormalities predominating;
- deaths between one month and one year (post-neonatal infant mortality rate), in which SIDS, infections (particularly respiratory) and accidents are major causes.

2.3 *Morbidity*

(a) Accidents

Data on the nature and extent of these are limited. Most accidents would not lead to hospital admission although many may go to accident and emergency departments. Data from these departments on cause of admission are not routinely available so a special local survey would be required.

(b) Infections

The register of notifiable diseases held by the environmental health department is a useful source of information on trends. GPs will have information on consultations as a result of infectious diseases. Some GP practices are 'sentinel practices' for the Royal College of General Practitioners and record the reasons for consultations each month. This allows the early stages of an epidemic to be picked up. It would be possible to set up such local sentinel practices. Advice on this can be obtained from your local public health medicine department. Vaccination and immunization ratios are inverse indicators of the likelihood of morbidity due to some infectious diseases and are available routinely.

(c) Congenital abnormalities

Information on congenital malformations by type and district is routinely available. Some local authorities and health authorities hold handicap, disability or disease registers of children with a congenital abnormality known to them.

3 MODIFIERS TO HEALTH EXPERIENCE

3.1 *Socio-economic*

The infant mortality rate, in particular the post-neonatal component, is affected by social deprivation. This is at least in part due to overcrowding, poor housing conditions and damp houses causing and encouraging infections. Because of this and other reasons, such as poor nutritional state, children from deprived backgrounds are more at risk from infectious diseases. They are also less likely to be vaccinated against them.

Accidents are much more common in socially deprived areas. Congenital abnormalities are also more likely in poorer families.

Sources of information
Social class, unemployment rate, number on housing benefit, car ownership, level of basic amenities and housing tenure type can all indicate
levels of social deprivation. Census-derived composite scores include
the Jarman and Townsend, both of which are available at ward level;
the former will also be available at practice level.

3.2 Environmental

The environment of the home, in terms of hazards and conditions, is
the major danger to children of this age. Dampness and cold increase
the risk of respiratory disease as does atmospheric pollution within the
home in the form of cigarette smoke. Accidents are encouraged by a
poorly designed or maintained home environment.

The amount of fluoride in the water supply may influence the amount
of tooth decay later. Fluoridation of the water supply has been shown,
at a population level, to reduce dental decay.

Sources of information
The quality of public sector housing may be known to the local housing
department. Otherwise a local survey will be required. Health visitors
may also be a good source of information on housing quality and home
environment safety levels.

3.3 Ethnic

Some congenital abnormalities are commoner in Asian children (e.g.
microcephaly, a syndrome causing mental impairment). This is thought
to be because of high rates of consanguinity (marriage between close
relatives). The infant mortality rate is also higher in children born to
women from India, the Caribbean and particularly Pakistan. Most of this
is accounted for by deaths in the first month of life, which are probably
caused by low birth-weight, small maternal stature, a large number of
previous children and consanguinity. The first two are associated with
social deprivation. The post-neonatal component is high in children
born to women themselves born in Pakistan; this is a reflection of social
deprivation.

Evidence suggests that in some ethnic groups within the Asian population infant feeding practices are detrimental to subsequent dental health.

Sources of information
Census data provide a breakdown of the number of households headed
by a person born in the New Commonwealth or Pakistan. This is routinely available at district level and can be broken down to ward level
and enumeration district. Unfortunately this does not give information

on those women born in this country who would still be considered as part of an ethnic minority group. The 1991 census should provide more useful information as it asked a question on self-perceived ethnic group membership.

Other sources of information on the ethnic composition of your local population include local community group leaders and the Community Relations Council. They can provide information on country of origin, language and religious background of ethnic minority groups. This type of information is essential for a more effective understanding of the needs of ethnic minority groups.

3.4   *Cultural*

The prevalence of breast feeding, age at weaning, the acceptability of vaccinations and attendance at child surveillance clinics may all be influenced by the local culture, independently of class influences.

The position in which children sleep has been shown to be related to the likelihood of sudden infant death; those children who sleep on their stomach have been shown to be at greater risk. The mode of placement of children may be culturally determined.

Sources of information
Local knowledge may hint at the issues but anthropological and sociological studies and consumer surveys will be required to provide more accurate information. Advice on these can be obtained from your public health medicine department.

4   HEALTH RESOURCES

The health resources available to this group include those listed below.

Within the individual
At this age it is difficult to see what health resources there are within an individual that are amenable to improvement.

Within the family
● family income;
● education of the family members;
● support from other members of the family;
● communication within the family;
● time and energy to teach the child.

Within the community
● church and other religious community groups;
● local health-related pressure groups;

- social support networks;
- babysitting circles;
- child-minders;
- community spirit;
- neighbourliness.

Health service
Health education/promotion:
- mother and baby groups;
- parent-held child health records;
- health education campaigns, e.g. vaccination campaigns;
- community development.

Primary care:
- child surveillance service;
- vaccination and immunization service;
- health visitors;
- community clinics;
- well baby clinics.

Secondary care:
- neonatology;
- paediatric service;
- community paediatrics;
- accident and emergency service.

Local authority
Housing department:
- provision of high quality, well designed public sector housing;
- prompt repair of public sector housing, including treatment for damp;
- system of medical rehousing for poor housing conditions;
- rehousing for homeless families.

Social services department:
- family worker schemes;
- advice on benefits;
- provision of day nurseries;
- facilities for children in care.

Private sector
- provision of high quality, well designed private sector housing;
- available and accessible recreational facilities for mothers and babies;
- child-minding.

Voluntary sector
- NSPCC day centres and family workers;
- associations for disabled children, e.g. MENCAP, Down's Syndrome Association etc.

5 MODIFIERS TO USE OF SERVICES

5.1 Socio-economic

It has been shown that working-class families make much more use of accident and emergency services as well as much more use of the GP at night, particularly for ill children. Mothers from working-class areas are less likely to make use of preventive services for children, such as vaccination and immunization, and child surveillance clinics.

5.2 Environmental

Access to services is reduced without access for pushchairs and prams. The availability of good public transport networks improves access to facilities. Even in households with a car the mother often does not have use of it during the day.

5.3 Ethnic

Health education material concerning child health is needed, in some areas, in languages other than English. Forms of communication other than writing, e.g. videos or drama, may be appropriate if there is low literacy in any language. Interpreters may be required if there are mothers who do not speak or understand English well.

6 SERVICE OPTIONS IN PRIMARY CARE

1 Child surveillance by GPs, which
   - includes both opportunistic and call and recall elements;
   - is supported by a system of continuing education for doctors on the child health list;
   - is carried out in collaboration with the district health authority;
   - includes a domiciliary service, if appropriate.
2 Vaccination and immunization service, which
   - includes both opportunistic and call and recall elements;
   - includes a domiciliary service if appropriate.
3 Oral rehydration programme. This is a programme to educate mothers on how to treat diarrhoea in their infants with a simple rehydration solution. Oral rehydration could prevent many of the hospital admissions for dehydration due to diarrhoeal illness.
4 Well baby clinics. These combine child surveillance, immunization and health education for parents in one session.
5 Play facilities and crèche facilities in GP surgery.
6 Assessment of home safety by health visitors.

7 Hiring of safety equipment.
8 Primary care team involvement with other agencies, e.g. in child abuse case conferences – liaison between the primary care team and social workers, NSPCC workers, education workers and the police.
9 Support groups for mothers of disabled children or other children with special needs.
10 Mother and baby groups for all mothers.
11 Employment of link workers in areas with large numbers of people from an ethnic minority group.

8 | LIFE STAGE:
FROM ONE TO
FOUR YEARS

1 INFLUENCES ON HEALTH

The chances of dying fall dramatically after the first year of life and only begin to rise substantially in the late thirties. However, the GP consultation rates suggest a high morbidity rate in this stage. Although pre- and perinatal influences are still exerting an effect on the health of this group, the health of the pre-school age group is influenced to a greater extent than that of younger ages by their social and environmental circumstances. Accidents and violence are major causes of death in this age group.

Mortality

Nationally the major causes of death in this age group are:
1 Congenital abnormalities.
2 Accidents and violence.
3 Diseases of the nervous system.
4 Malignant neoplasms (cancers).
5 Infections.

6 Diseases of the respiratory system.

7 Diseases of the circulation.

8 Endocrine, nutritional, metabolic and immunity disorders (a collection of related, mostly rare, abnormalities, but including diabetes).

9 Sudden infant death syndrome (SIDS).

10 Diseases of the digestive system.

These causes account for 93 per cent of deaths in this age group.

Morbidity

(a) GP consultations

Data are available on GP consultations for various categories of diseases from studies carried out by the Royal College of General Practitioners[1] in 1981–2. The data are analysed for age group 0–4 years as opposed to 1–4 years so this must be borne in mind. Overall the consultation rate is six times higher in this age group than in older children. The commonest reasons for attendance were, in order of descending magnitude, as follows:

- diseases of the respiratory system;
- diseases of the nervous system;
- infections;
- ill-defined conditions;
- skin diseases;
- accidents and violence;
- digestive system disorders;
- diseases of the genito-urinary system;
- mental disorders (mainly trivial).

(b) Hospital admissions

Hospital admission rates are as much a reflection of bed availability, referral rates and admission procedures as an indicator of need. However, they can provide useful information on how need is currently being translated into provision of hospital services. In children many of the admissions are theoretically preventable. The commonest diagnoses for episodes of admission in children in this stage in 1988 in the North Western Regional Health Authority were:

- asthma;
- respiratory infections;
- convulsions;
- diarrhoea;
- tight foreskin;

- glue ear (secretions caused by long-term respiratory infection build up in the ear, leading to hearing loss);
- head injury;
- swollen tonsils.

These eight diagnoses accounted for only about a quarter of admission episodes.

(c) Disability

It is important to have information not only on the prevalence of diseases but also on the long-term effects of them. Children with long-standing illnesses and disabilities have increased health and social service needs. Surveys have shown that the commonest types of disability in this age group are:

- behaviour disability or disorder;
- disability associated with personal care and continence;
- disability associated with communication and locomotion.

There are a very large number of causes of disability in young children, including congenital abnormalities, inherited diseases and brain damage occurring during or after birth. The last is usually caused by infections of the brain (e.g. meningitis and encephalitis) or head injury.

(d) Oral health

National studies have shown that children in the North of England have the worst dental health in England and Wales. District based surveys confirm this. They also show differing disease levels between districts, thus highlighting geographic pockets of poor dental health. The majority of these are in the North Western Region. Over the past 20 years dental health has improved in the child population. However, this trend appears to be slowing or even reversing.

2 SOURCES OF INFORMATION ON HEALTH

2.1 Demography

The number of pre-school children in a community is available from census data with annually updated projections by ward and district. The percentage of residents who are in this age group can be produced easily for small areas, which can then be aggregated into urban and rural populations.

2.2 Mortality

Mortality rates are routinely available by age group and cause groups and for some individual causes. The information is usually two or three years out of date but this is not important as any changing trends in death rates occur slowly.

2.3 Morbidity

(a) General

GP consultation rates are available as above, but these are national figures and somewhat out of date now. More local data could be obtained from local GPs but these would need to be collected, collated and analysed locally. Hospital admissions data from KES (Körner Episode System) can provide information on numbers, residence and diagnoses for children admitted to hospital for each district. However, KES refers only to episodes of admission, not to the history of admissions of particular individuals.

(b) Accidents

The police keep records of serious traffic accidents. A special survey of the accident and emergency department could provide information on the nature and extent of these plus some other types of accidents. However, the decision to take a child to the accident and emergency department depends on many factors, including nearness of the department, availability of the GP, perceived seriousness of the accident and perceived benefit of attending.

(c) Infections

Certain infectious diseases are notifiable and as such the medical practitioner attending any person whom he or she suspects of suffering from this condition must notify the authorities. The current list of notifiable diseases affecting this age group includes: meningitis; tetanus; encephalitis; TB (tuberculosis); polio (poliomyelitis); diphtheria; whooping cough (pertussis); mumps; rubella (German measles); measles; food poisoning; dysentery; infective jaundice; scarlet fever; some other very rare infectious diseases.

Despite notification being a legal requirement only a proportion of cases are notified, so the system is not useful for assessing need in terms of absolute numbers. However, it gives useful information on trends and is used to predict epidemics.

(d)   Congenital abnormalities

These can cause morbidity and disability in this age group. Sources of information include handicap or disability registers held by the local authority or health authority. The education department may also have a list of *statemented children,* i.e. those assessed under the 1981 Education Act as having special educational needs.

(e)   Disability

Information on the prevalence of disabled pre-school children is hard to obtain accurately. Possibilities include:

Extrapolation from national studies   The results of the OPCS study[2] of disability in children can be extrapolated to the local population. This national study showed a prevalence of 21 per 1000 children aged 0–4 years having some disability. Thirteen per 1000 had behavioural disabilities, six per 1000 had problems with personal care and the same number had continence problems. Five per 1000 had disabilities with locomotion and five per 1000 with communication. These ratios were higher for boys than girls. Two-thirds had multiple disabilities.

Local data   There may be a local disability or handicap register kept by the local authority or health authority. This records children known to the services who are suffering from a disability. It is unlikely to be complete, particularly in the pre-school age group.

Another option is to carry out a local survey. This will be difficult and expensive to perform and may not give any better information than extrapolation from national surveys. Advice on how to carry out such a survey can be obtained from the local public health medicine department.

Some voluntary groups associated with disabled children may have some information on prevalence in the area. They may also have more qualitative information on service provision quality and gaps. They may be a resource for obtaining further information with advice from public health physicians.

(f)   Oral health

No national data are collected for pre-school children. Local data may be available at district level from the community dental service. Under the new general dental practitioner (GDP) contract children are able to register with a GDP, who will receive a capitation fee. In this situation it ought to be possible to obtain rates for the number of children in each age group who have registered with a local GDP.

3   MODIFIERS TO HEALTH EXPERIENCE

3.1   Socio-economic

(a)   Accidents

Deaths due to accidents in children show the highest social class gradient of any cause of death. There are many postulated reasons for this, including:

- poor home design;
- overcrowding at home;
- lack of safe playing areas outside the home;
- less income to spend on safety equipment;
- less supervision of children.

(b)   Infections

A lack of basic amenities, overcrowding and poor nutrition can all contribute to the higher level of infectious diseases in socially deprived families.

Damp housing increases the risk of respiratory disease in children, as does the presence of a smoker in the house, which is known to be more likely in a working-class household. Respiratory disease in the parents is associated with an increased risk in the child. This may be because the diseased parent coughs and infects the child. Respiratory disease in adults is more common in working-class and socially deprived areas.

Sources of information
Social class, unemployment rate, number on housing benefit, car ownership, level of basic amenities and housing tenure type can all indicate levels of social deprivation. Composite scores include the Jarman and Townsend, both of which are available at ward level; the former will also be available at practice level.

3.2   Environmental

Home accidents are the commonest accidents in this group and so the safety of the home environment is important. In addition accidents outside the home are beginning to rise. These are related to the proportion of children with safe playing space. In general this means the proportion of homes with gardens and the number and situation of municipal parks.

The amount of fluoride in the water will affect the level of tooth decay. An efficient and effective public health measure is the fluoridation of public water supplies at one part per million.

Sources of information
Information on safe playing areas may be available from the housing department and the leisure services department of the local authority.

3.3 Ethnic

Tuberculosis is much more common in Asian children. There is evidence that congenital abnormalities are more common in children born to women born in the Indian sub-continent, particularly women from Pakistan. This may relate to high levels of consanguinity (marriage between close relatives).

Sources of information
Census data will provide information on the place of birth of the head of household, e.g. the proportion of households in an area that are headed by someone born in the New Commonwealth or Pakistan. This is also available at ward level. Unfortunately the census does not give information on those people born in this country who would still be considered as part of an ethnic minority group. The 1991 census should provide more useful information as it asked a question on self-perceived ethnic group membership.

Other sources of information on the ethnic composition of your local population include local community group leaders and the Community Relations Council. They can provide information on country of origin, language and religious background of ethnic minority groups. This type of information is essential for a more effective understanding of the problems and needs of ethnic groups.

3.4 Cultural

There is very little information at present on the different cultural influences on child-rearing and its consequences for health. Some studies have suggested that where extended family members live locally grandmothers play a very important role.

The position in which children sleep has been shown to be related to sudden infant death, i.e. the risk is higher in children who sleep on their stomach. The mode of placement of children in bed may to some extent be culturally determined.

Dietary factors involved in poor oral health are culturally influenced. Infant feeding practices may also be culturally determined (e.g. the use of a sweetened dummy). The norms for dental self-care may be culturally determined.

Sources of information
Special anthropological and sociological studies could provide this type of information. Involving local parents' perspectives in planning or

purchasing teams who are assessing need in this age group should highlight local cultural influences on health.

4 HEALTH RESOURCES

The health resources available to this group include those listed below.

Within the individual
- health curiosity;
- health-promoting habit development;
- self-esteem.

Within the family
- education of family members;
- family support networks;
- family income;
- communication within the family.

Within the community
- church and other religious community groups;
- health-related pressure groups;
- social support networks;
- sharing child-care;
- babysitting circles;
- pleasant and stimulating environment to live in.

Health service
Health education/promotion:
- mother and pre-school child groups;
- parent-held child health records;
- health education campaigns;
- community development.

Primary care:
- child surveillance service;
- vaccination and immunization;
- health visitors;
- community clinics;
- community dental service.

Secondary care:
- paediatric service;
- community paediatrics;
- accident and emergency service.

Local authority
Housing department:
- provision of high quality, well designed public sector housing;
- prompt repair of public sector housing, including treatment of damp
  housing;

- system for medical rehousing because of poor housing conditions;
- rehousing for homeless families;
- a system of appropriate housing allocation for families with children, e.g. not placing young children in a flat above the second floor.

Social services department:
- family support worker schemes;
- advice on benefits;
- crèches;
- respite care for disabled children;
- nightsitting service;
- services for children in care.

Planning department:
- permitting developments that take into account the needs of children.

Education department:
- number and location of pre-school nursery places.

Private sector
- provision of high quality, well designed private sector housing;
- available and accessible recreational facilities for mothers and young children;
- nurseries and child-care facilities.

Voluntary sector
- NSPCC day centres and family workers;
- associations for disabled children, e.g. MENCAP, Down's Syndrome Association etc.;
- support for carers of young or disabled children;
- hospice provision for terminally ill children;
- support for bereaved parents.

5   MODIFIERS TO USE OF SERVICES

5.1   Socio-economic

It has been shown that working-class families make much more use of accident and emergency services as well as much more use of the GP at night, particularly for ill children. Mothers from working-class areas are less likely to make use of preventive services for children, such as vaccination and immunization, and child surveillance clinics.

It is important for leisure facilities to be within easy reach of children from socially deprived backgrounds, who are less likely to have access to a private garden. Good public transport facilities to recreational and health care facilities are very important in socially deprived areas where car ownership is low.

5.2 Environmental

Facilities without disabled access cannot be used by many disabled children.

5.3 Ethnic

Health education material concerning child health is needed in languages other than English, particularly in areas with large numbers of mothers who do not read English well. Alternatively, videos or drama may be used to communicate with people with low literacy in English. Interpreters may be required if there are mothers who do not speak or understand English well.

6 SERVICE OPTIONS IN PRIMARY CARE

1 Child surveillance by GPs, which
   - includes both opportunistic and call and recall elements;
   - is supported by a system of continuing education for doctors on the child health list;
   - is carried out in collaboration with the district health authority;
   - includes a domiciliary service, if appropriate.
2 Vaccination and immunization service, which includes:
   - both opportunistic and call and recall elements;
   - a domiciliary service, if appropriate.
3 Oral rehydration programme. This is a programme to educate mothers on how to treat diarrhoea in their infants with a simple rehydration solution. Oral rehydration could prevent many of the hospital admissions for dehydration due to diarrhoeal illness.
4 Well baby and well child clinics. These provide an opportunity for child health surveillance, immunization and health education for parents in one session.
5 Play facilities and crèche facilities in GP surgery.
6 Assessment of home safety by health visitors.
7 Hiring of safety equipment.
8 Primary care team involvement with other agencies, e.g. in child abuse case conferences, and liaison between the primary care team and social workers, NSPCC workers, education workers and the police.
9 Support groups for mothers of disabled children or other children with special needs.
10 Mother and child groups for all mothers.
11 Employment of link workers to liaise with women from ethnic groups.
12 Close liaison between the general dental service and the community dental service.

REFERENCES

1 Royal College of General Practitioners (1986) *Morbidity Statistics from General Practice: Third National Study 1981–82*. London: OPCS, HMSO.
2 Bone, M. and Meltzer, H. (1989) *The Prevalence of Disability among Children*. OPCS surveys of disability in Great Britain Report 3. London: HMSO.

9 LIFE STAGE: FROM FIVE TO 14 YEARS

1 INFLUENCES ON HEALTH

Overall the death rate in this age group is very low. The excess of male deaths seen in all age groups is beginning to become more pronounced, with over one-third more deaths in males than in females. Accidents are by far the most common cause of death in this age group and predominantly occur outside the home; accidents to younger children predominantly occur in the home. They are over twice as common in boys as in girls. The commonest accidents to cause death are motor vehicle and other transport accidents, followed by recreational accidents. Research has shown that in most transport accidents the children are pedestrians or cyclists rather than passengers in the vehicles. Suicide and self-inflicted injury are also beginning to figure in the mortality data in the later ages of this age group. Cancers, particularly leukaemia and bone cancer, are the second commonest cause of death. Deaths as a consequence of congenital abnormalities still figure quite highly.

Mortality

Nationally the major causes of mortality are as follows.

1 Accidents and violence.
2 Cancer.
3 Diseases of the nervous system.
4 Congenital abnormalities.

These four causes account for 75 per cent of deaths in this age group.

Morbidity

(a)   GP consultations

This age group consults the GP six times less frequently than the younger children. The commonest reasons for consultation during the Royal College of General Practitioners study in 1981–2 (cited in Chapter 8) were very similar to those in the younger age group, with respiratory diseases and infections being the most common. Accidents are only the fifth commonest in the table but it is to be expected that in many accidents the child will be taken straight to the casualty department rather than to the GP, and so these figures will not indicate the true scale of the burden of accidents to the level of ill-health in this age group.

The top ten diagnoses for which the GPs were consulted in 1981–2 are shown below.

1 Diseases of the respiratory system.
2 Infections.
3 Diseases of the nervous system and sense organs.
4 Symptoms, signs and ill-defined conditions.
5 Accidents and violence.
6 Diseases of the skin.
7 Muscle and bone diseases.
8 Diseases of the digestive system.
9 Diseases of the genito-urinary system.
10 Mental disorders.

(b)   Hospital admissions

Hospital admissions are as much a reflection of referral rates, admission policies and bed availability as a measure of morbidity. They provide useful data, however, particularly in children, where many hospital admissions are theoretically preventable with appropriate primary care treatment.

The commonest episode diagnoses in this age group in the North Western Region are as follows.

1 Chronic tonsillitis/swollen tonsils.
2 Abdominal pain.

3 Head injury.
4 Glue ear (secretions caused by long-term respiratory infection build up in the ear, leading to hearing loss).
5 Asthma.
6 Dental caries.
7 Tight foreskin.
8 Deafness.
9 Appendicitis.

These nine diagnoses only account for less than a quarter of admissions in this age group.

(c) Disability

It is important to have information not only on the prevalence of diseases but also on the long-term effects of them. Children with long-standing illnesses and disabilities have increased health and social service needs. Surveys have shown that the known prevalence of most types of disability increases once the child has gone to school. This may be because the extra rigours of school life bring to light the minor disabilities. It may also be because more of them are brought to the attention of the services available within schools, such as the school medical service. The commonest types of disability in this age group are shown below.

1 Disability associated with behaviour.
2 Communication difficulties.
3 Intellectual disabilities.
4 Problems with continence.
5 Problems with locomotion.

Overall, behaviourial disorders and disabilities with intellectual functioning are more prevalent in the older ages of this age group, with disabilities associated with personal care and continence becoming less prevalent.

There is a very large number of causes of disability in children, including congenital abnormalities, inherited diseases and brain damage occurring during or soon after birth. Another cause is head injury.

(d) Oral health

National studies have shown that children in the North of England have the worst dental health in England and Wales. District based studies confirm this. They also show differing disease levels between districts and highlight pockets of very poor oral health. Over the past 20 years dental health has improved in the child population, but this trend appears to be slowing or even reversing.

Dental decay and gum disease are not the sum total of oral health. It has been recommended by dentists that all children be examined for orthodontic problems around the age of twelve.

Health-related behaviour

Towards the end of this age range certain behaviours that affect health are sometimes adopted. Many of these, e.g. smoking, alcohol consumption and illicit drug taking, are more prevalent in the higher age groups but they may start in the early teens; this is particularly so for solvent misuse.

Sexual activity may also commence within this age group, often bringing with its inherent pleasures consequences for health, such as unwanted pregnancies, sexually transmitted diseases and emotional problems. This is discussed in more depth in the next life stage.

2 SOURCES OF INFORMATION ON HEALTH

2.1 Demography

The number and residence of children in this age group are available, with annual projections.

2.2 Mortality

Mortality statistics are routinely available by cause, sex, district and age.

2.3 Morbidity

(a) Accidents and violence

The police keep records of road traffic accidents. Special surveys of accident and emergency departments should be carried out if it is felt that it would be useful to determine the extent and consequences of accidents in a community. The school medical service may have records of accidents occurring in schools and their consequences. Hospital data on accidents, suicide and self-inflicted injury are routinely available and will give useful data on accidents and violence severe enough to warrant hospital admission.

(b) Cancers

Hospital admissions data are available but difficult to interpret as it is likely that an individual with cancer will be admitted many times in a year and the data available are by admission episode and not by individual. This can lead to overcounting of cases.

Each regional health authority has a cancer registry, the exceptions being the four Thames regions, which share one registry. The registries can provide information on cases of cancer registered with them. Not all cases are on the register but the majority are. When someone dies of cancer the registry is informed, so information on deaths is the most accurate.

Collectively, GPs are a very good source of information on children with cancer in their practices. Despite cancer being the second commonest cause of death in this age group, the overall death rate is so low that it is still a very rare disease. It is therefore unusual for a GP to have any children on his or her list with cancer, but if all GPs in an area were surveyed it is likely that all children with cancer could be identified. It is unlikely that GPs will routinely collect these data for their own use but special surveys of GPs could assess the prevalence in an FHSA population.

(c) Congenital abnormalities

The number and type of congenital abnormalities are routinely available at birth but not at other ages.

(d) Disability

If information on the extent and nature of disabilities in a community is required the following may be useful sources of information.

Handicap registers Children with a disability, either physical or intellectual, may be recorded on a handicap register. These registers are kept by some local authorities and a few health authorities. They are not compulsory and their completeness varies from place to place.

The education department of the local authority The Education Act of 1981 requires that children with special educational needs are *statemented* and their special needs documented. This is then a source of information on intellectual and physical disability in an area. Again incompleteness is a problem with this source of data. The education department may also run special schools and the number of children attending will be relatively readily available. Further details on those attending may require a special survey.

The school medical service The school medical service can often be a very good source of information on the numbers of disabled children in schools and the level of disability. Some may even hold a register of children with disabilities.

Primary health care team GPs and other members of the team are likely to have a lot of information on disabled children on their caseload.

Special surveys Sources of information on disability are probably better for school-age children than for any other age. However, these sources can still be incomplete, even for children with severe disabilities and particularly for those with minor disabilities. Another problem may be that the information is not available in an accessible form. The only way to try to overcome this and more accurately to quantify the level of need in this area is to carry out a special disability survey. This can be time-consuming and expensive. However, some surveys have been done in some areas and it may be feasible to extrapolate their results to your own population.

The OPCS survey of disability in children (cited in Chapter 8) found a prevalence of disability of 38 per 1000 in children aged 5–9 years and 35 per 1000 in children aged 10–15 years. Overall the rates were higher for boys than girls and two-thirds had multiple disabilities. These rates can be used to assess the likely prevalence of disabilities in your area.

(e) Oral health

Nationally surveys of the dental health of the UK are conducted by OPCS. Surveys are carried out in one-year age bands from 5 to 15 years old. They have been conducted every ten years since 1973. The General Household Survey also includes some dental questions.

Locally, dental health surveys are carried out annually within health authority districts by the community dental service. These began in 1985/6. Five year olds, 12 year olds and 14 year olds are surveyed. Five year olds are surveyed every two years and 12 and 14 year olds every four years. The local results are available from the district dental officer of the community dental service in the district health authority.

3 MODIFIERS TO HEALTH EXPERIENCE

3.1 Socio-economic

As already mentioned for younger age groups, accidents show the clearest and largest social class gradient of any cause of death. The death rate from accidents in children from social class V families (families of un-skilled workers) is seven times that in children from social class I families (professional parents). Reasons for this include less access to safe play areas, less supervision of play and more miles travelled on foot than in a car. The last reason is important because research has shown that most accidents to children occur with the child as a pedestrian or cyclist rather than a passenger in a vehicle. In Manchester research showed that these accidents predominantly occurred on smaller residential roads rather than major roads. The more a child has to walk the larger his or her risk of being run over. It is to be expected that children from working-class families are less likely to be driven to and from school than middle-class children.

More children from social classes IV and V are likely to be living in high-rise flats, which increases the chances of falls as well as reducing the possibilities for supervision of outdoor play.

Damp houses and overcrowding increase the likelihood of infections, particularly respiratory infections. These are more common in socially deprived areas. Poor dental health also seems to be associated with social deprivation. Many factors are involved and the explanation is complicated.

Sources of information

Social class, unemployment rate, number receiving housing benefit, car ownership level, proportion of houses with basic amenities and housing tenure type can all indicate levels of social deprivation. Composite scores include the Jarman and Townsend, both of which are available at ward level; the former will also be available at practice level. Other indicators available from some housing departments include the number of children in council accommodation known to be 'living at a height', i.e. living above a certain floor level.

3.2 Environmental

(a) General

The physical environment is a very important factor in determining the likelihood of accidents occurring (e.g. the presence of derelict buildings, the proximity of railway lines, canals etc.). The safety of the road layout is also important (e.g. pedestrian crossings and in particular safe residential roads with devices for slowing down the traffic).

Whether the school age children in the practice or FHSA population live in an urban or rural area and the location of the schools is important. Children living in rural areas generally have further to travel to school but have easier access to safe playing areas, although there remain many environmental hazards in rural areas.

Other environmental risk factors include the presence of carcinogenic products from industry or the natural environment. These include radiation and radon gas, both of which may be associated with increased likelihood of childhood leukaemias. Other environmental hazards include atmospheric and water pollution.

Dental health is influenced by the level of fluoride in the public water supply.

(b) Housing

The immediate household environment is also important, as mentioned in relation to infectious diseases. Housing construction and design will influence the likelihood of damp developing as well as the risk of accidents within the home. Children living in high-rise buildings are less likely to be supervised at play and the risk of falling from a height is greater.

Sources of information

Various local authority departments are likely to have information on the physical environment (e.g. leisure services, highways department and the housing department). An alternative is to take a walk around the area and observe.

The environmental health department may have information about atmospheric pollutants, water pollution levels and atmospheric radiation levels. The housing department should have information on housing type and some indicators of the number of families with children in high-rise flats, in houses without gardens and in houses awaiting repair.

3.3 Ethnic

Areas with large numbers of children from an Afro-Caribbean background may encounter more children with sickle cell anaemia. Diseases with a higher prevalence in Asian children include TB and rickets.

Sources of information

The census is a source of information on the proportion of the household from ethnic groups, in that it records the place of birth of the head of household. Unfortunately this will not give information about people born in this country who consider themselves part of a minority ethnic group. The 1991 census should help as it contains a question on perceived ethnic group.

More information on language, religion and the country of origin of the ethnic minority groups in your area can be obtained by talking to the Community Relations Council or the local community leaders of those groups.

3.4 Cultural

There may be cultural differences in the rearing of children and the value placed upon particular services, regardless of class and ethnic group.

Towards the end of this age group there may be cultural differences in the area of unhealthy behaviours, such as smoking, alcohol consumption, illicit drug taking and sexual practices. The 'youth culture' seems to vary dramatically from place to place and even from year to year, so it is important to keep up to date with the changes.

Diet, particularly sugar intake, may be culturally determined and thus influence dental health. Norms for self-care of teeth and gums may well also be determined culturally.

Sources of information
Unfortunately, information on the local 'youth culture' is not readily available and must be sought out. Studies in schools, youth clubs and on the streets can yield valuable information but they are difficult to perform with the necessary scientific rigour. Your public health medicine department can give you advice on this. Talking to field-workers, such as teachers, school nurses and in particular youth workers and drug workers, can be very informative in this area.

4 HEALTH RESOURCES

Health resources available to this group include the following.

Within the individual
- risk awareness and level of risk aversion;
- educational level;
- decision-making skills;
- assertiveness;
- self-esteem.

Within the family
- family income;
- family support networks;
- education of other family members;
- family communication.

Within the community
- shared child-care;
- community support networks;
- community spirit;
- local health-related pressure groups;
- church and other religious community groups;
- pleasant environment to live in.

Health service
Health education:
- in schools, particularly relating to life skills, training to assist in making choices regarding substance misuse and in the area of sexuality;
- education of children and parents regarding safety in the home and on the road;
- dental health education.

Primary care:
- emergency, on call GP service;
- school medical service;
- community clinics;
- community dental service.

Secondary care:
- accident and emergency service;
- paediatric service;
- orthodontic service;
- oral surgery.

Local authority
Housing department:
- availability of high quality public housing with gardens or other safe play areas;
- prompt treatment of damp housing conditions;
- policy regarding the rehousing of homeless families;
- policy regarding housing allocation and transfer of families with children.

Leisure services department:
- availability of leisure facilities accessible to socially deprived areas.

Education department:
- personal and social education in schools (PSE) which concentrates on developing decision-making skills;
- health education in schools;
- youth and community service;
- educational welfare service;
- school meals provision.

Highways department:
- provision of safe roads, particularly in residential areas.

Planning department:
- permitting schemes that take into account the needs of children.

Probation service
- crime prevention initiatives.

Private sector
- transport networks to school and recreational facilities;
- availability of leisure facilities;
- water fluoridation level.

5 MODIFIERS TO THE USE OF SERVICES

5.1 Socio-economic

Research has shown that children from socially deprived areas make more use of the emergency services, in both primary and secondary care. Whether this is over and above that accounted for by the obvious increase in ill-health (particularly accidents) is unclear.

It is important for leisure facilities to be within easy reach of children from socially deprived backgrounds, who are less likely to have access to a private garden. Good public transport facilities to recreational and health care facilities are very important in socially deprived areas where car ownership is low.

5.2 Environmental

Disabled children require disabled access to services.

5.3 Ethnic

Some children from minority ethnic backgrounds may not speak English well, and either they or their parents will require interpreters. Health education material may need to be produced in more than one language.

6 SERVICE OPTIONS IN PRIMARY CARE

The options include the following.

1 Open access service for minor injuries.
2 Crèche in GP surgeries.
3 Support groups for carers of children with special needs.
4 Counselling service for emotionally distressed children, particularly teenagers.
5 Liaison between the school medical service and the primary health care team – in particular in children with special needs, e.g. disabled children or those from homeless families.
6 Liaison between the community dental service, primary care team and general dental practitioners.
7 Bereavement counselling for families in which a child dies.
8 Terminal care at home.

10 | LIFE STAGE: FROM 15 TO 24 YEARS

1 INFLUENCES ON HEALTH

This age group is a time of transition between childhood and adulthood in which the behaviour of the individual is a most important determinant of their present and future health status. Important risky behaviours are often more prevalent in this age group than others. Risky behaviours include smoking, drunkenness, violence, illicit drug taking, poor dietary habits and multiple sexual partners. It can be a time of tremendous physical, mental and emotional growth and such a time of change can bring confusion and poor mental health.

The major cause of death remains accidents, probably contributed to by some of the risky behaviours mentioned above. Suicide and self-inflicted injury are also major causes of death. Cancers remain a large contributor to the death rate in both sexes and deaths from circulatory diseases (heart disease and strokes) are beginning to emerge by the end of the age group.

Once this stage in the life cycle is reached it is not appropriate to group together male and female causes of ill-health in a community as their health experiences are so different. This is in part due to the fact that women have reached child-bearing age and much of their

'morbidity' or use of health services is associated with fertility, pregnancy and childbirth. Women have traditionally involved themselves
less in risky behaviours than men, although recent research suggests
this is much less the case now, particularly with regard to smoking
and drunkenness.

Mortality

The major causes of death nationally in this age group are as follows.

Male
1 Accidents and violence.
2 Suicide and self-inflicted injury.
3 Cancers.
4 Diseases of nervous system.
5 Circulatory diseases.
6 Respiratory diseases.
7 Mental disorders.
8 Congenital abnormalities.
9 Endocrine, nutritional and metabolic.

Female
1 Accidents and violence.
2 Cancers.
3 Suicide and self-inflicted injury.
4 Circulatory diseases.
5 Diseases of nervous system.
6 Respiratory diseases.
7 Congenital abnormalities.
8 Endocrine, nutritional and metabolic.
9 Infections.

In men these account for 98 per cent of deaths in this age group. Accidents alone account for over 45 per cent. In women these account for
85 per cent of deaths with accidents accounting for just under a quarter.
Men are nearly four times more likely than women to die from an
accident and three and a half times more likely to die from a suicide
attempt than women.

Morbidity: GP consultations

Data from the GP study in 1981–2 (cited in Chapter 8) show a fairly high
consultation rate for this age group, 35 per cent higher for women than
for men. As can be seen, much of the increase in attendance among
women can be accounted for by attendance for services relating to their
fertility.

The top ten reasons for which these young adults attended the GP were as follows.

Male

1 Respiratory disease.
2 Accidents and violence.
3 Skin diseases.
4 Infections.
5 Symptoms, signs and ill-defined conditions.
6 Diseases of nervous system.
7 Muscle and bone diseases.
8 Digestive diseases.
9 Mental disorders.
10 Diseases of genito-urinary system

Female

1 Family planning services.
2 Respiratory diseases.
3 Pregnancy care.
4 Diseases of genito-urinary system.
5 Symptoms, signs and ill-defined conditions.
6 Skin diseases.
7 Infections.
8 Accidents and violence.
9 Diseases of nervous system.
10 Prenatal care.

2 SOURCES OF INFORMATION ON HEALTH

2.1 Demography

The numbers and sex distribution of this age group are available routinely at district and ward level, allowing mapping of the adolescent and young adult population. Annual projections are also available.

2.2 Mortality

The numbers and rates of deaths by cause and age group are available routinely for each district health authority. This enables comparisons to be made with other districts. The number of deaths in this age group remains small and so caution should be taken in looking at areas smaller than district health authorities.

Suicides will be known to the local coroner. Deaths from traffic accidents and some other accidents will be known to the police. Most deaths from cancers will be registered with the local cancer registry.

2.3 Morbidity

(a) General

GP consultation rates are available nationally for 1981–2 from the Royal College of General Practioners' study mentioned above. Local data on the prevalence and incidence of diseases in GP practices would be of great value in describing the burden of ill-health in the community but would need to be collected, collated and interpreted locally.

KES (Körner Episode System) can provide information on hospital admissions in this age group, although this is in part a reflection of bed availability, referral rates and admission policies as well as a reflection of ill-health.

(b) Accidents and violence

The local police force will have information on accidents reported to them as well as some incidents of violence.

The accident and emergency department collects information on all accidents seen but it would generally require a special survey to collate the information at DHA or FHSA level and to interpret it.

(c) Mental health

Information regarding people who have attempted suicide (parasuicide) and have been admitted to hospital is available from the hospital data system (KES). It would be difficult to obtain accurate information on those who were not admitted to hospital. Other information is available from attenders of psychiatric services, either in- or outpatients, or day hospital attenders. Most people with mental health problems are never admitted to hospital, however, so more reliable information can be obtained from community staff, such as GPs, community psychiatric nurses, health visitors and mental health social workers.

Another valuable source of information is self-help groups like MIND, tranquillizer support groups, agoraphobic support, etc. However, many people with minor mental health problems and some with major mental illness are not in contact with any service, and special community surveys are required to assess the true need for services within a community. There are several well used and validated survey techniques that can detect emotional and psychological distress in a community. One widely used instrument is Goldberg's *General Health Questionnaire*.[1,2] An alternative to carrying out your own survey is to extrapolate from other community surveys.

(d)   Homelessness

The number of homeless has been increasing at an alarming rate, particularly among young adults. Benefit changes have led to much poverty in this group. A recent study in Manchester concluded that young, single, homeless people showed evidence of great emotional distress and general poor mental health as well as poor physical health. Information on young homeless people in your area may be available from the following.

1 The local authority housing department. They are obliged to rehouse homeless families, which includes pregnant women or other priority groups, including those deemed to be 'vulnerable'. This does not generally include single homeless people and only very few local authorities will hold information on them.
2 Charities such as CHAR and Shelter.
3 GPs may be aware of homeless people on their lists. Most of these will be in temporary accommodation. However, there is a problem that many homeless people are not registered with GPs.
4 The probation service may have information on the proportion of their clients who are homeless, including those in temporary accommodation.
5 Welfare rights officers may also collect information on those who come to them reporting homelessness.

(e)   Cancers

The regional cancer registry will have information on people who have been diagnosed as having cancer. This is available for each district health authority population and in the future it may be possible for information to be presented by FHSA area and GP practice. The registry in the North Western Region holds information on age, sex, residence, cancer site and date of death where appropriate. Studies of attenders of self-help groups and hospices may be able to provide more qualitative data on the experiences of people with cancer in your area.

(f)   Oral health

National surveys of the dental health of those aged from 15 to 24 years are available. They are carried out every ten years by the OPCS. The first was performed in 1968. The General Household Survey also contains questions on dental health. Local data may also be available from your local community dental service, particularly regarding young adults with special needs.

2.4 Health-related behaviour

(a) Illicit drug use

Information about this group is hard to come by because the illegality of the activity means it is hidden from most people, including health service planners. Some information from national studies is known about users of some substances; for example, most heroin users start in their late teens and early twenties, the majority are male, unemployed and from socially deprived areas.

Local sources of information include the following.

1 Drug misuse database. Each regional health authority has set up a database on drug misusers. In the North Western Region this is held by the Drug Research Unit at Prestwich Hospital.
2 Notifications of addicts to the Home Office available by police area.
3 GPs.
4 Attendances at community drug teams.
5 Attendances at needle exchange schemes.
6 Talking to field-workers, particularly outreach workers.
7 Relatives' support groups.
8 Drug users' support groups.

The first two are routinely available; the others will require special surveys. The first two sources will predominantly provide information on opiate users (heroin, morphine etc.) whereas it is just as important to know about other drug use, particularly injecting drug use (e.g. amphetamine and cocaine use). As services have less to offer stimulant users they are less likely to attend them. Outreach services are extremely valuable at providing information to and from this group.

(b) Alcohol use

Many young people go through a phase of drinking heavily and inappropriately. Information about the nature and extent of the problem in your area is likely to be hard to come by. Possible sources include the following.

1 Local councils on alcohol. For example, in the North Western Region this is the Greater Manchester and Lancashire Council on Alcohol.
2 Community alcohol team or community drug team.
3 Health promotion department.
4 Probation service regarding alcohol-related crime.
5 Local police department regarding alcohol-related crime and alcohol-related accidents.
6 Self-help groups, e.g. Alcoholics Anonymous.
7 Breweries.

8 Talking to field-workers, e.g. teachers, youth workers, outreach drugs workers.

It is unlikely that any of the above can give a complete picture of the problem and special surveys in schools, colleges and youth clubs, at work or in the community may need to be undertaken.

(c)   Sexual practices

This age group is at a time of exploration and it is to be imagined that many young people are intermittently sexually active at this time. Unfortunately there is little reliable information on young people's sex lives. This information is now necessary because of the threat AIDS poses to the public health. Some studies have suggested that in some areas over half of those aged 14 years have been involved in some sexual activity, that many do not use any contraception and that even fewer use barrier methods.

Sexually transmitted diseases are an important cause of morbidity in this life cycle stage. They can have short- or long-term effects on health and include the following.

Disease	Possible long-term effects
gonorrhoea	salpingitis (infection of the fallopian tubes) and infertility
syphilis	paralysis, insanity
genital herpes	if in pregnancy may necessitate a caesarian section
anal warts	linked to cervical cancer
AIDS	death
cervical cancer	infertility and death

The commonest result of unprotected sexual intercourse is pregnancy, and the numbers of unwanted pregnancies can be seen as an indicator of the use of reliable contraceptive methods. Indicators of the extent of unhealthy consequences of unprotected intercourse include:

- number of abortions in this age group and rate compared with the national and regional average;
- teenage birth rate, i.e. births between the ages of 15 and 19 years;
- number of people who are HIV positive by risk group;
- cases and rates of other sexually transmitted infections, e.g. gonorrhoea and syphilis.

These data should all be available from your Regional Health Authority.
Indicators of health-promoting behaviour include:

- attendances at family planning clinics and type of contraception used (numbers and trends);
- condom sales locally (numbers and trends).

Special surveys may be required for these although condom sales locally may be available from sales representatives of companies selling the condoms.

Cervical cancer deaths and cases from the cancer registry probably relate to the pattern of sexual activity a few years ago as well as reflecting the relative success or failure of the cervical cytology screening process. The number of positive smears is therefore a poor indicator of sexual activity as there are too many other contributing factors to the development and discovery of a positive smear.

3 MODIFIERS TO HEALTH EXPERIENCE

3.1 Socio-economic

The social class distribution within an area is likely to influence many of the factors affecting the health of this age group. Mortality from accidents and violence and most cancers shows a marked association with social class. Illegal drug use is more likely in socially deprived areas, particularly those with high unemployment rates.

Studies of alcohol consumption have shown a particular pattern of drinking in socially deprived areas, with more heavy 'binge' drinking than elsewhere. Poorer mental health has been shown to be associated with unemployment and social deprivation. Working-class women have been shown to be particularly susceptible to depression. Working-class mothers in general have more children at a younger age, have more low birth-weight children and are more likely to be late attenders at antenatal classes. Those with a low income have less money to spend on a healthy diet, particularly fresh fruit and vegetables.

Sources of information
Unemployment rate, social class distribution, percentage of families with no car, percentage of houses without basic amenities, percentage of families on income support, housing tenure areas and percentage on housing benefit are all available indicators of relative social deprivation. Composite scores such as the Jarman and Townsend exist down to ward level. Jarman scores are now available at practice level.

3.2 Environmental

Environmental factors likely to influence the health experience of this age group in your area include the following.

(a) Urban versus rural

Whether the practice, DHA or FHSA is in a rural or urban area will influence health. Generally rural areas show a different pattern of accidents. Inner-city areas will generally have more deprivation as well as a more mobile population. Homeless people are likely to migrate to towns.

(b) Employment

Are the main employers heavy industry, small businesses, light industry or farming? The answer to this will dictate to some extent the level of work accidents and mental health associated with work. The overall availability of work will affect both known and hidden unemployment rates, which will affect both physical and mental ill-health.

Some jobs are particularly associated with some diseases (e.g. bladder cancer in those who work with aniline dyes). Other potential hazards to health from work in this age group include:

- accidents in heavy industry, farming and the construction industry;
- stress associated with boring, repetitive jobs;
- 'sick building' syndrome;
- repetitive strain injury in clerical staff;
- low back strain in labouring and nursing.

Some occupations are by their very nature dangerous, such as prostitution.

Sources of information
Whether one of your major employers is associated with known occupational hazards should be available from your public health medicine department or the environmental health department of the local authority.

The local office of the Department of Employment should have information on the major employers in your area as well as up-to-date unemployment rates by age.

Local knowledge and outreach workers are invaluable in providing information to and from prostitutes.

(c) Housing type and standards

Damp housing will increase the risks of respiratory diseases. High-rise, deck access flats are associated with poor mental health and could result in consequent high parasuicide and suicide rates, as well as increased drug and alcohol consumption.

Sources of information
The local authority housing department should have information on the types of housing in an area.

(d)   Transport networks

Poor public transport systems will limit access to recreational amenities, cheap shops, friends and relatives as well as health service facilities.

Sources of information
Local knowledge is important. The local authority and health authorities may have information on travelling times to services from various places in the district. Otherwise they will need to be calculated using information from the transport providers. Community transport groups and schemes such as 'dial-a-ride' may be able to provide information.

(e)   Environmental hazards

As well as at work, people can be exposed to environmental hazards in their daily lives, such as atmospheric particle pollution, radon gas, carcinogens in the atmosphere and high nitrate levels in the water supply.

Sources of information
The local authority, particularly the environmental health department, may have local information on environmental hazards.

3.3   Ethnic

There may be ethnic differences in the rates of substance misuse but this cannot be assumed. Both Asians and Afro-Caribbeans are more likely to be victims of violence. Some diseases are more prevalent in ethnic minorities in this age group than in the white population. These include accidents in all, some blood diseases in Afro-Caribbeans and TB in Asians.

Sources of information
The place of birth of every head of household is routinely available every ten years from the national census. This is available down to ward level. Place of birth is not useful in areas where most of the members of ethnic groups are second and third generation immigrants who were born in the UK. Information on ethnic group membership should be more accurate since the 1991 census, which included a question on the self-perceived ethnic group membership of each household. Other information about the ethnic minority group (e.g. language spoken, religion, country of origin) can be obtained by speaking to the Community Relations Council or representatives of the ethnic group, such as community leaders.

3.4   Cultural

The levels and types of substance misuse are associated with both national and local culture. Types of drugs used, level of injecting and amount of sharing all seem to be influenced by the local drug using culture. Strict Muslims are not supposed to drink alcohol. The smoking of cannabis (ganja) is of religious significance to some Rastafarians.

New trends in behaviour can emerge very rapidly (e.g. skateboarding or acid house parties) and it is wise to keep one's ear to the ground for the latest local developments in 'youth culture'. It has been suggested that there is a 'working-class culture' in which living for the moment is more important than investing in the future. It has also been suggested that this is not a different culture but a rational response to a life over which one has little control. Whatever the reasons the result is that more health-damaging behaviour may be sanctioned by the community (e.g. smoking, not using contraception). Another implication of this outlook is that preventive services may not be valued as highly.

Sources of information
Anthropological and sociological surveys of local values and beliefs about health and illness, as well as surveys on the limitations to peoples' possibilities for healthy choices, could be very illuminating in this area.

Different ways of involving local young people in the debate over what the local health priorities are will need to be explored in order to develop a needs based service.

4 HEALTH RESOURCES

The health resources available to this group include:

Within the individual
● self-esteem;
● awareness of risk and level of risk aversion;
● assertiveness and ability to resist peer group pressure;
● decision-making skills;
● communication skills;
● educational level.

Within the family
● family income;
● level and quality of communication between family members;
● family support;
● education of other family members.

Within the community
● community support networks;
● availability of healthy work;
● community spirit;
● safe and pleasant leisure areas;
● pleasant and stimulating environment to live in.

Health service
Primary care:
- counselling services;
- community clinics;
- family planning service by GPs;
- family planning clinics by health authority;
- community drug team;
- community alcohol team or equivalent;
- self-help groups for drug misusers and their families;
- self-help groups for alcohol misusers and their families;
- community dental service for people with special needs.

Secondary care level:
- counselling service;
- abortion service;
- drug dependency clinic;
- psychiatric service for drug and alcohol misusers;
- dental hospital;
- hospital dental service;
- adolescent psychiatry unit;
- gynaecology;
- trauma and orthopaedics;
- accident and emergency department;
- genito-urinary medicine clinics, including HIV counselling.

Local authority
Housing department:
- non-stigmatizing services for young homeless, single and families.

Education department:
- adult education courses.

Leisure services department:
- adult recreational facilities.

Probation
- alcohol education courses;
- drug education courses;
- social skills training;
- support for homeless offenders;
- other crime prevention initiatives.

Voluntary sector
- self-help groups for drug and alcohol misusers and their families;
- counselling services for drug misusers;
- counselling services for alcohol misusers;
- halfway hostels;
- therapeutic communities;

- family planning services;
- abortion services;
- abortion counselling services;
- Samaritans;
- self-help counselling groups;
- AIDS/HIV positive counselling services;
- drop-in centres for young unemployed or homeless;
- hostels for homeless young people;
- soup kitchens.

5   MODIFIERS TO USE OF SERVICES

5.1   Socio-economic

A lack of disposable income and less access to a car mean that services need to be provided locally in socially deprived areas.

5.2   Environmental

Disabled young people's use of services will be affected by their physical access to them through ramps etc.

5.3   Ethnic

Most Asian women are willing to see only a female doctor, so access to a woman doctor at family planning clinics and antenatal clinics is vital. People whose first language is not English will require interpreters and educative material in the appropriate language. Videos or drama may be a more appropriate medium for educating people with low literacy levels.

5.4   Cultural

Roman Catholics are usually opposed to abortion and, in theory, to the use of artificial methods of contraception.

6   SERVICE OPTIONS IN PRIMARY CARE

1 A high-quality family planning service with a wide range of options available, including:
   - large number of GPs able to fit the coil and diaphragm;
   - separate sessions as family planning clinics;
   - availability of women doctors;

- availability of crèches at family planning sessions;
- availability of interpreters and relevant health education literature where appropriate;
- no practice where all the GPs refuse to provide a contraceptive service or to refer for abortion;
- availability of special family planning clinics for men;
- availability of special family planning clinics for young people;
- availability of the 'morning after' pill.

2 Services for drug users and alcohol misusers might include:
- GPs who are willing to treat illicit drug users and problem alcohol users;
- specific programmes of treatment for illicit drug users or problem alcohol users run by the primary care team;
- GPs willing to prescribe methadone on a withdrawal or maintenance basis;
- GPs/primary care teams with specific programmes of withdrawal for benzodiazepine users;
- GP liaison with the community drug team.

3 Care in pregnancy includes:
- GPs on obstetric list providing shared care;
- home delivery service by GPs;
- community midwives on primary care teams;
- antenatal clinics in GP surgeries:
  - ○ with availability of women doctors,
  - ○ in the evening for working mothers,
  - ○ with interpreters as necessary,
  - ○ with crèches,
  - ○ and with health education, including dental advice, from midwives.

4 Mental health for young people: the employment or placement in the GP surgery of a community psychiatric nurse or clinical psychologist to provide emotional support and counselling to young people in distress.

5 Accident and violence service: an open access wound dressing/stitching service by nurses and GPs.

REFERENCES

1 Goldberg, D. P. (1978) *Manual of the General Health Questionnaire*. Slough: National Foundation for Education and Research.
2 Goldberg, D. P. and Williams, P. (1988) *A User's Guide to the General Health Questionnaire*. Slough: National Foundation for Education and Research.

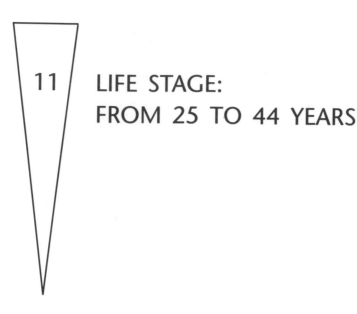

11 / LIFE STAGE: FROM 25 TO 44 YEARS

1 INFLUENCES ON HEALTH

The death rate begins to rise again in this life cycle stage, being 67 per cent higher than in the previous stage. The excess of male deaths continues but to a lesser degree, with the male death rate being 35 per cent higher than the female death rate.

The health experience of women in this age group is predominantly associated with their role as child-bearers. Problems associated with family planning, pregnancy and childbirth, as well as diseases of the reproductive organs, figure highly; that is, women's health experience is largely associated with gynaecological and obstetric issues.

Accidents remain a major cause of death in both sexes but malignant neoplasms (cancers) have overtaken accidents as the top cause of death.

In men, genetic and life-style factors interact to cause mortality in this age group. Smoking-related diseases begin to figure highly, although leukaemias are still the commonest cancer, with lung cancer the second commonest. Ischaemic (or coronary) heart disease is already a major cause of death in men and in some areas even outranks accidents. Suicide remains an important cause of mortality.

Mortality

The major causes of mortality nationally in this age group are as follows.

Male
1 Cancers (particularly leukaemia, then lung, then brain).
2 Accidents.
3 Ischaemic heart disease.
4 Suicide.
5 Digestive system diseases.
6 Nervous system diseases.
7 Respiratory diseases.
8 Mental disorders.
9 Congenital abnormalities.

Female
1 Cancers (particularly breast, then cervix, then leukaemia).
2 Accidents.
3 Suicide.
4 Nervous system diseases.
5 Digestive system diseases.
6 Ischaemic heart disease.
7 Respiratory diseases.
8 Mental disorders.
9 Congenital abnormalities.

In both men and women these account for 80 per cent of deaths at this life cycle stage. Cancer causes under 20 per cent of male deaths in this age group and nearly 50 per cent of female deaths.

Morbidity

The GP consultation rates are much the same in this age group as for the previous, with women still consulting more than men. The commonest reasons for consultation nationally in 1981–2 were as follows.

Male
 1 Respiratory diseases.
 2 Musculo-skeletal problems.
 3 Accidents and violence.
 4 Ill-defined conditions.
 5 Skin diseases.
 6 Nervous system diseases.
 7 Infections.
 8 Mental disorders.
 9 Digestive system diseases.
10 Diseases of heart and circulation.

Female
1 Respiratory diseases.
2 Genito-urinary diseases.
3 Family planning.
4 Ill-defined conditions.
5 Pregnancy care.
6 Mental disorders.
7 Musculo-skeletal problems.
8 Skin diseases.
9 Infections.
10 Nervous system diseases.

2 SOURCES OF INFORMATION ON HEALTH

2.1 Demography

The number of people in this age group is available routinely at district
and electoral ward level with annual projections. The fertility rate among
women of this age group is also routinely available at district level and
thus can be compared between districts.

2.2 Mortality

The death rates for all causes, for each classification of disease and for
certain individual causes by sex and age group are available for each
district health authority. The data can be made available at ward level.
However, death in this age group remains a rare event. Consequently
ward level death rates for particular causes will have been compiled from
very small numbers of actual deaths. This can make comparison of death
rates open to much misinterpretation (see Chapter 3).

Information on cancer deaths can be obtained from the local regional
cancer registry. The district public health medicine department should
know the whereabouts of this in your area. Deaths from accidents and
violence will be known to the police. Suicides will be known to the local
coroner.

2.3 Morbidity

(a) General

GP consultation rates are available nationally (cited in Chapter 8) for
1981–2. Local data on the prevalence and incidence of diseases in GP
practices in your FHSA would be of great value in describing the burden
of ill-health in the community. This would need to be collected, collated
and interpreted locally.

KES (Körner Episode System) can provide information on hospital admissions in this age group. It must be remembered, however, that admission rates are partly a reflection of bed availability, referral rates and admission policies as well as indicators of ill-health. KARS (Körner Aggregated Returns System) can provide information on users of community services in this age group.

(b)   Cancers

Each regional health authority has a cancer registry, with the exception of the four Thames regions, which share one. This can provide information on all people registered with cancer who are resident in each DHA. If the information in the cancer registry is postcoded then it will be possible to produce statistics by FHSA or DHA area. In theory the information is available by ward or even GP practice, but again the small numbers involved make comparisons between districts and between years potentially misleading. The postcoding relating to small areas is less accurate than that relating to districts. The information may be between one and two years out of date.

(c)   Morbidity associated with sexual activity and fertility

Premalignant (precancerous) changes in the cervix   Cancer of the cervix is a preventable cause of death in women. It is associated with sexual activity, in that virgins do not get it. It is not necessary to be promiscuous to suffer from cervical cancer. Smoking increases the risk of suffering from it.

A recent study in the North Western Region has shown that the vast majority of women who died of cervical cancer in the region had not received a smear test in the last five years. A smear test performed properly can pick up the changes that occur in the cells of the cervix before cancer develops.

Every DHA and FHSA now runs a call and recall system for a cervical cytology service for women between the ages of 20 and 64 years of age. Women are invited to attend for screening every three or five years. Many women aged between 25 and 44 are consulting services for care in pregnancy, childbirth and family planning so that smears can be carried out opportunistically. GPs can play a vital role here. There is, however, no substitute for systematic screening of eligible women. Information on uptake rates within the target population of the GP practice is now routinely available.

Genito-urinary diseases   Cystitis, thrush (candida infection) and other infections associated with sexual activity are common causes of morbidity in this age group, particularly in women. They account for many consultations in primary care. There are also many self-help remedies and support groups that attempt to address these problems. The pro-fusion of self-help groups may be a reflection of the health service's inability to address these problems to the satisfaction of the community.

Information on the incidence and prevalence of these conditions is most likely to be available from surveys of women attending specialist services, such as family planning clinics, genito-urinary medicine clinics (formerly sexually transmitted disease clinics) and in particular well women clinics or centres. Local surveys in primary care may also produce useful information.

Antenatal care   Although pregnancy is a normal physiological process antenatal surveillance has been shown to improve the health of both the mother and the baby. The vast majority of babies in this country are born in hospital, with antenatal care being either totally at the hospital or shared by the GP.

Major morbidity associated with pregnancy is now rare but minor morbidity is less so. Information on major morbidity will be available from hospital admissions to maternity hospitals. Information on minor morbidity is unlikely to be routinely available but may be available from the hospital service, community midwives or the GP.

(d) Mental health

Mental health problems are an important cause of morbidity in this age group. Emotional distress associated with child-rearing, relationships, be-reavement and work is a common experience. Most people cope without any assistance from primary or secondary care services. The assessment of the extent of minor psychiatric morbidity will therefore depend on community surveys. There are several well used and validated survey instruments that can detect emotional and psychological distress within a community. One such is the Goldberg questionnaire cited in Chapter 10. Your local public health medicine department should be able to advise you on these. An alternative is to extrapolate from national or regional surveys. Your public health medicine department should have information on these.

Information on those whose mental health problem leads them to hospital admission will be available from the hospital data system (KES). Other information is available on attenders of psychiatric services as outpatients or of the day hospital. These data would need to be collated and interpreted locally.

As most people with mental health problems are not admitted to hospital more reliable information can be obtained from community staff, such as community psychiatric nurses, GPs, health visitors and mental health social workers. These professionals may all be part of the primary care team. Information from some of these field-workers may be available from KARS data from the health service. Another valuable source of information on psychiatric morbidity is self-help groups, such as MIND, tranquillizer support groups, agoraphobia support groups, etc. They can give information on the perspective of users of services.

(e)   Oral health

National surveys of the dental health of those aged from 25 to 34 years and from 35 to 44 years are available from the OPCS. They have been conducted every ten years since 1968. The General Household Survey also contains some questions on dental health. Local data may be available from your community dental service, particularly regarding adults with special needs.

3   MODIFIERS TO HEALTH EXPERIENCE

3.1   Socio-economic

The social class distribution of an area is likely to influence the health experience of that community in this age group as in any other. Overall, cancer is much commoner in people in social class V than in the professional classes. The only two common cancers where this is not the case are breast cancer and malignant melanoma (a form of skin cancer). The differences in rates cannot be entirely explained by the observed differences in health-related behaviours like smoking. Cervical cancer is commoner in working-class women yet they are much less likely to have received a smear in the past five years than middle-class women. Mortality from accidents and violence is markedly increased among working-class people.

Poor mental health has been shown to be associated with increased levels of unemployment and social deprivation. Depression has been found to be much more prevalent among working-class women than among middle-class women or men.

The prevalence of smoking is much higher in working-class communities, as is the prevalence of smoking-related diseases such as respiratory disease. Low income families spend less on fresh fruit and vegetables.

Sources of information
Unemployment rate, social class distribution, percentage of families with no car, percentage of houses without basic amenities, percentage of families on income support, type of housing, percentage on housing benefit and number of single parent families are all available indicators of relative social deprivation. Composite scores such as the Jarman and Townsend exist and are routinely available at district and ward level. Jarman scores should be available at practice level.

3.2 Environmental

(a) Urban versus rural

Whether the practice, FHSA or DHA population is rural or urban will influence health. Generally rural areas show a different pattern of accidents. Inner-city areas will show more deprivation and have a more mobile population. Homeless people are likely to migrate to towns. Women from urban areas have been shown to be more likely to be depressed than women from rural areas.

Sources of information
Local knowledge of the area is important.

(b) Work

The working environment is an important modifier of the health experience of this age group. Potential hazards at work are very large in number and include:

- accidents in heavy industry, construction and farming;
- exposure to dangerous chemicals and other compounds, e.g. coal dust, asbestos, radiation;
- repetitive strain injury and 'sick building' syndrome in office workers;
- muscle and bone strains in labourers, nurses etc;

Mental health problems can be associated with work and have been shown to be increased with unemployment.

Sources of information
Local knowledge of the major employers in the area can be obtained from the local office of the Department of Employment. Whether a major employer in your area is associated with known occupational hazards should be available from the public health medicine department or the environmental health department of the local authority. The local office of the Department of Employment will have up-to-date unemployment rates.

(c) Housing type and standards

Environmental hazards in the home that may modify the health experience of this age group include the presence of radon gas and, for non-smokers, living with a heavy smoker. Both of these increase the risk of lung cancer.

Damp housing is associated with an increased prevalence of respiratory diseases. High-rise, deck access flats are associated with poor mental health and could result in high parasuicide (attempted suicide) and successful suicide rates as well as increased rates of drug and alcohol use.

Sources of information
The local authority housing department should have information on the types of housing in the area as well as other useful indicators of quality of life in public sector housing, such as the waiting list for repairs, the turnover rate and the percentage of voids (empty houses). The environmental health department may have information on the level of radon gas in the area.

(d)   Transport networks

Poor public transport systems will limit access to recreational amenities, cheap shops, friends and relatives as well as to health service facilities. This is particularly true for those on low incomes and for women in this age group, who are likely to have small children with them.

Sources of information
Local knowledge is important. The local authority and health authorities may have information on travelling times to services from various places in the district. Otherwise they will need to be calculated using information from the transport providers. Community transport groups and schemes such as 'dial-a-ride' may be able to provide information.

(e)   Environmental hazards

As well as at work, people can be exposed to environmental hazards in their daily lives. Examples include atmospheric particle pollution, radon gas, other carcinogens in the atmosphere and high nitrate levels in the drinking water supply.

Sources of information
The local authority, particularly the environmental health department, may have information on known environmental hazards (e.g. levels of atmospheric and water pollution).

3.3   Ethnic

Asians and Caribbeans are more likely to be victims of violence. Overall, cancer is less common in Asians. The prevalence of smoking and heavy drinking is less among Asians but ischaemic heart disease is more common. This may in part be due to the fact that diabetes is much more prevalent among Asians. Hypertension is six times more common in Afro-Caribbeans than in the white population.

Sources of information
The place of birth of every head of household is routinely available every ten years from the national census. This is available down to electoral ward level. Place of birth is not useful in areas where most of the members of ethnic groups are second and third generation immigrants born in the UK. Better information should be available from the 1991 census, which asked a question on self-perceived ethnic group membership of the household.

A national database on the health experience of ethnic groups is in the process of being set up in London. This should provide useful data in the future. Further, more qualitative, information on the lives of the ethnic group members in your area (e.g. language spoken, religion and country of origin) should be available from the Community Relations Council or from community leaders of the ethnic groups.

3.4 Cultural

In some social groups it has been suggested that single parenthood is culturally considered the norm. This may have implications for the health of the lone parent. Recreational activities may to some degree be culturally determined, such as the extent to which people go to the local pub for entertainment and the amount of exercise taken, although class and income differences are more likely to be of relevance. Local beliefs and values about ill-health and the benefits of treatment may differ.

Sources of information
Anthropological and sociological surveys would be needed to produce this information, but local knowledge may hint at some of the issues.

4   HEALTH RESOURCES

Health resources potentially available to this age group include those presented below.

Within the individual
- self-esteem;
- awareness of risk and level of risk aversion;
- assertiveness;
- decision-making skills;
- communication skills;
- education.

Within the family
- family income;
- level and quality of communication between family members;

- family support;
- willing and able carers for the sick and disabled.

Within the community
- community support networks;
- babysitting circles;
- parent support groups;
- availability of healthy work;
- community spirit;
- church and other religious community groups;
- pleasant and stimulating environment to live in.

Health service
Health education/promotion:
- women's health;
- work-related health;
- dental health;
- stress management;
- decision-making skills;
- community development.

Primary and community care:
- family planning service by GPs;
- family planning clinics by health authority;
- health promotion clinics;
- cervical cytology service by GPs and collaboration with the cervical cytology service organized by the health authority;
- well woman centres;
- well woman clinics;
- well man clinics;
- self-help groups, e.g. Look After Your Heart, smoking cessation groups;
- counselling services, e.g. community psychiatric nurses, clinical psychologists;
- coronary heart disease facilitators;
- community midwives;
- health visitors;
- MacMillan nurses;
- community dental service for adults with special needs.

Secondary care:
- general medical and surgical services;
- accident and emergency service;
- obstetric and gynaecology service;
- antenatal clinic;
- maternity hospital;
- fertility clinics;
- abortion service;

- oncology services;
- hospital dental service.

Local authority
Housing department:
- services for homeless families and single homeless;
- provision of high quality public sector housing.

Education department:
- adult education courses.

Leisure services department:
- encouragement of healthy exercise and recreation.

Transport services department:
- subsidizing private sector bus services in areas of social need.

Probation service
- alcohol education courses;
- drug education courses;
- life skills courses;
- crime prevention initiatives.

Voluntary sector
- parent support groups;
- child-care facilities;
- counselling services, e.g. Relate;
- mental health support groups;
- Samaritans;
- abortion services;
- pregnancy advice centres;
- self-help groups for cancer sufferers;
- MacMillan nurses.

5 MODIFIERS TO THE USE OF SERVICES

5.1 Socio-economic

Working-class women have been shown to be less likely to use preventive services, such as screening clinics and antenatal clinics. Whether this is because of a decreased perception of personal benefit or an increased perception of the cost of attending such services is not always clear. Lack of access to a car, lack of disposable income for public transport costs, no crèche facilities and taking young children on public transport all increase the costs to the woman of availing herself of these preventive services. It has been shown that appropriately designed local services are more likely to be used by women from socially deprived areas.

5.2   Ethnic

Most Asian women will neither undress in front of nor allow an internal examination by a male doctor. Interpreters may be necessary for women whose first language is not English. Information about services may have to be in languages other than English. Videos or drama may be a more appropriate means of giving information for those with low literacy levels in English.

5.3   Cultural

Religious beliefs may alter service utilization. Roman Catholics are in principle opposed to abortion for whatever reason and in some cases to artificial methods of contraception. They may therefore require access to advice on natural methods of birth control and are likely to refuse tests that aim to pick up congenital abnormalities in order to abort the fetus. Jehovah's Witnesses will not accept transfusions of blood or blood products.

6   SERVICE OPTIONS IN PRIMARY CARE

6.1   Health promotion in primary care

(a)   Well woman centres/clinics

These are clinics that encourage women to take more control over their own and their family's health. They arose in response to the recognition that women are the main informal health educators in the community and that often their own personal health needs were not being met by a predominantly male run health service. They are not just health screening clinics. They should involve:

- the taking of a detailed life-style history;
- discussion about the main health risks to the woman from both her perspective and the perspective of the health professional;
- personal health education counselling;
- advice about present ill-health if appropriate (in studies in Manchester it has been found that two-thirds of attenders have current health problems, which they felt they could not take to mainstream health services);
- screening tests as appropriate, e.g. cervical cytology, breast self-examination, blood pressure screening;
- development of self-help groups.

(b)   Well man clinics

These can be run with the same philosophy as well woman clinics but often they place more emphasis on pre-symptomatic screening and less on becoming an active participant in the health professional–patient relationship.

In this age group screening for hypertension (high blood pressure) is valuable, particularly among Afro-Caribbean men. Advice on a healthy life-style is also appropriate. The general screening of blood cholesterol levels has not been found to be beneficial and should be confined to those with a strong family history of ischaemic heart disease associated with high serum cholesterol levels.

(c)   Smoking cessation groups

These can develop out of the well person clinics or independently of them. Some models have been found to be effective, particularly if a doctor is involved, but long-term follow-up is required.

(d)   Other health promotion clinics (e.g. Look After Your Heart)

These offer general advice in a supportive environment that aims to reduce the level of coronary heart disease risk factors and to encourage a healthy life-style, i.e. good diet, regular exercise, no smoking and a moderate alcohol intake. They may be linked to formal call and recall screening programmes for identifying alterable coronary risk factors (see below).

(e)   Coronary heart disease facilitators

Coronary heart disease facilitators are generally health professionals working in primary care teams to facilitate the organization of a health promotion and screening programme specifically to identify those at high risk of developing coronary (ischaemic) heart disease. It is important if a practice or the health authority employs a facilitator that he or she is well trained, not professionally isolated and works as part of the primary care team. He or she should work with clearly agreed protocols for screening services. Formal call and recall screening programmes to identify and modify alterable CHD risk factors have yet to be shown to be cost-effective.

(f)   Community development

Some people say that all of the above attempts to improve the health of a community are inappropriate for those living in socially deprived areas. This is because they all depend on individuals recognizing that health is a priority in their life. For people on low incomes just surviving from day to day takes up the majority of their energy, time and money.

The community development approach focuses on working within the community's priorities and on attempting to assist people in meeting what they perceive to be their immediate needs, including the requirements to improve their own and their family's health. These perceived needs of the community may differ from the health professional's defined need. In areas of social deprivation it may be appropriate for community development workers to be employed at practice, DHA or FHSA level.

(g) Cervical cytology

GPs and other primary care staff are well placed to carry out cervical cytology screening. As women are high users of the health service in this age group it is likely that most smears will be carried out as a result of opportunistic screening. No opportunity should be missed to offer a woman who has never been screened a cervical cytology smear test. However, there is little benefit to be gained from offering additional screening to women who are already happily complying with the national call and recall programme. Recent research in the North West suggests that many women who die of cervical cancer have never been screened.

6.2 Care in pregnancy

Options include:

- GPs on the obstetric list providing shared care;
- home delivery service by GPs;
- GP obstetric unit;
- antenatal clinics in GP surgeries:
  - o with a woman doctor,
  - o with a crèche for other children,
  - o run by community midwives,
  - o in the evening for working women,
  - o with an interpreter if necessary,
  - o which offers health education.

6.3 Family planning

A high quality family planning service providing a large range of family planning options with:

- large numbers of GPs able to fit the coil and diaphragm;
- availability of women doctors;

- availability of crèches;
- availability of interpreters and relevant health education material where appropriate;
- special clinics for men;
- availability of the 'morning after' pill.

There should be no area where women do not have access to a family planning service or abortion service because of the religious views of GPs.

6.4 Mental health

Options include:

- community psychiatric nurse attached to a GP practice;
- counselling sessions run either separately or as part of well person clinics;
- stress management courses in the practice;
- development of self-help groups by the primary care team.

6.5 Accidents

Provision of an open access wound dressing service by the GP or a nurse.

12 / LIFE STAGE: FROM 45 TO 64 YEARS

1 INFLUENCES ON HEALTH

The number of deaths rises greatly in this life cycle stage. The death rate is over ten times higher in men in this age group than in the previous one and nine times higher among women. Mortality in this age group accounts for 20 per cent of all male deaths and 12 per cent of all female deaths.

The male death rate increases by age at a higher rate than the female death rate and is consequently 70 per cent higher than the female rate in this age group. From this life cycle stage onwards the big four killers are coronary (also called ischaemic) heart disease, cancers, cerebrovascular disease (strokes) and respiratory diseases (predominantly chronic bronchitis, emphysema and pneumonia). Coronary heart disease accounts for about 40 per cent of deaths in men in this age group but for less than a fifth of deaths in women in this age group.

Although much of the mortality risk is determined by age and genetic factors, a substantial proportion of the deaths in this age group associated with these diseases is potentially preventable, as some of the risk factors identified can be modified by changes in behaviour or changes in the environment.

Other than the differences in the cancers experienced by the different sexes the causes of death are more similar between men and post-menopausal women, although men do experience them at a greater rate than women.

Women consult their GPs more than men and the excess can no longer be accounted for by problems associated with child-bearing and fertility. Some of the excess may be accounted for by symptoms associated with sexual activity and the menopause. Respiratory diseases remain a major reason for consultation but problems with muscles, bones and joints are now the most common reason in women and the second most common in men. Women consult more often than men with problems of mental health.

Mortality

The major causes of mortality nationally are:

Males
 1 Ischaemic heart disease.
 2 Cancers.
 3 Respiratory disease.
 4 Cerebrovascular disease.
 5 Diseases of digestive system.
 6 Accidents and violence.
 7 Other lung and heart diseases.
 8 Suicide.
 9 Nervous system diseases.
10 Metabolic/endocrine diseases (mainly diabetes).

Females
 1 Cancers.
 2 Ischaemic heart disease.
 3 Cerebrovascular disease.
 4 Respiratory disease.
 5 Diseases of digestive system.
 6 Nervous system diseases.
 7 Accidents and violence.
 8 Other lung and heart diseases.
 9 Metabolic/endocrine diseases (mainly diabetes).
10 Suicide.

These account for 95 per cent of deaths in men and 93 per cent of deaths in women. Cancers cause half of female deaths and a third of male deaths in this age group.

The five commonest sites of fatal cancers are:

Males
1 Lung (39%).
2 Large bowel (11%).
3 Stomach (7%).
4 Oesophagus (5%).
5 Pancreas (4%).

Females
1 Breast (28%).
2 Lung (17%).
3 Large bowel (10%).
4 Ovary (9%).
5 Cervix (4%).

Morbidity

The top ten reasons for consultation with GPs in 1981–2 were:

Males
1 Respiratory diseases.
2 Musculo-skeletal problems.
3 Diseases of circulation.
4 Ill-defined conditions.
5 Nervous system diseases.
6 Accidents and violence.
7 Skin disorders.
8 Digestive disorders.
9 Mental disorders.
10 Infections.

Females
1 Musculo-skeletal problems.
2 Respiratory diseases.
3 Ill-defined conditions.
4 Mental disorders.
5 Diseases of the circulation.
6 Genito-urinary diseases.
7 Nervous system diseases.
8 Accidents and violence.
9 Skin disorders.
10 Digestive disorders.

2 SOURCES OF INFORMATION ON HEALTH

2.1 Demography

The number of males and females in this age group and annual projections are routinely available down to electoral ward level. The

household composition is also available from census data every ten years.

2.2 Mortality

Death rates for all causes, for each classification of disease and for certain individual causes are routinely available by age, sex and district. They can also be produced at ward level, but for some causes the small numbers involved can lead to likely misinterpretation of the data (see Chapter 3).

Deaths from cancers can be obtained from the local regional cancer registry. Your local public health medicine department will be able to inform you of its address. If the information in the registry is postcoded then it is theoretically possible to produce statistics by each FHSA or other locality. It is also possible to produce the information for smaller areas, but for many cancers the small numbers involved make comparisons between districts and between time periods open to misinterpretation (see Chapter 3).

2.3 Morbidity

(a) General

Routine data sources include:

- Körner Episode System (KES), which can provide information on hospital admissions in this age group – it must be remembered, however, that admission rates are as much a reflection of bed availability, referral rates and admission policies as a measure of need;
- Körner Aggregated Returns System (KARS), which will provide information on users of some health authority community services.

National GP consultation rates (source cited in Chapter 8) are available for the year 1981–2. More up-to-date and local data from GP practices would be very useful. This would need to be collected, collated and interpreted locally. The General Household Survey is a national survey carried out annually. It can provide national data on the prevalence of long-standing illness and limiting long-standing illness, and restricted activity in the previous 14 days. The information is available by age group. The information is national.

(b) Cancer

A list of people diagnosed as having cancer is available from the cancer registry for each district health authority and theoretically should be available by FHSA or other locality. This could be aggregated into sex and age bands. It could also be provided at practice level but comparisons between practices and trends would be difficult because of the small numbers involved.

(c)   Circulatory diseases (Heart disease and strokes)

As these are the major preventable causes of death and disability in this age group it is important to have information about the local incidence and prevalence of these conditions. Unfortunately this is difficult to obtain as many people have no obvious symptoms of these diseases until a very late stage.

Ischaemic heart disease (coronary heart disease) leads to angina (chest pain on exertion), myocardial infarctions (heart attacks) and arrhythmias (disturbed rhythm of the heart). An ECG (electrocardiogram) and sometimes other tests are required to be sure of the diagnosis. Strokes are one manifestation of cerebro-vascular disease that is more likely in people with high blood pressure (hypertension). High blood pressure is not a disease in itself but increases one's risk of both stroke and ischaemic heart disease.

Sources of information
Ischaemic heart disease   With angina (chest pain on exertion):

- hospital admission data;
- information from outpatient departments (in some cases this will be available routinely, in others special studies will be required);
- GP data (will need to be collated specially).

With a 'heart attack' (myocardial infarction): as long as this is accompanied by symptoms most people in this age group would be admitted to hospital, so hospital admission data by age group and area would be useful.

With an arrythmia (disturbed heart rhythm): some information will be available from hospital data and from local GPs but it will be incomplete as not all arrhythmias cause symptoms.

Work medical examination and occupational health records may pick up undiagnosed ischaemic heart disease.

Strokes (cerebrovascular disease)   Most major stroke sufferers are admitted to hospital and thus information can be obtained from the hospital data systems. Minor strokes or major ones where there is sufficient community support may not be admitted to hospital. Your area may even have a community stroke team. If so this team, GPs and the community services may have information on people who have suffered a stroke in your area. The community services collect some data routinely, which are collated as KARS data. Information from GPs would probably have to be specially collected and collated locally.

(d) Disability

Whatever the underlying illness, purchasers and planners of health services need to know the level of any residual disability. Possible sources
of information on disability include those mentioned above under the
specific diseases as well as extrapolation from national or regional figures
on the prevalence of disability.

The national disability survey carried out by OPCS[1] in 1988 found a
prevalence of disability in the community of:

- 79 per thousand in the 45–49 age group;
- 106 per thousand in the 50–54 group;
- 155 per thousand in the 55–59 group;
- 205 per thousand in the 60–64 group.

A survey of disability levels from whatever cause was carried out by the
Arthritis Research Council[2] in Calderdale and published in 1988. It found
that 66 people per thousand in the 16–64 years age group reported difficulties or dependence on others. Three-quarters of these were in the
45–64 years age group. Thirteen per thousand reported relying on others,
with eight per thousand reliant on help from others for important daily
activities such as washing, dressing, toileting and getting in and out of
bed. Again, the vast majority of these were in the 45–64 years age group.
Rheumatic and neurological disorders were major causes of physical
impairment in the community, as were heart and respiratory disorders,
which also caused people to be confined to their homes.

Local disability surveys could be carried out at DHA, FHSA or practice
level if appropriate, but are probably unlikely to reveal significantly different results from those above.

The disablement resettlement officer in the local job centre may be a
source of information on numbers of disabled people in this age group
who are looking for work.

(e) Coronary heart disease risk factor prevalence

The above sources of information are useful for assessing prevalence for
the purpose of planning or purchasing local services. From the public
health perspective the principle of screening is either to identify those
at risk of developing a disease in order to prevent it or to pick up the
disease at an early stage in order to improve the outcome of treatment.

Apart from the difficulties of screening for the actual disease, it may
be too late to intervene once ischaemic heart disease is present. Therefore most coronary heart disease prevention programmes attempt to
identify those who are at greater risk of developing the disease rather
than those who already suffer from it, in the hope that reducing the risk
factors will prevent the disease from developing.

The major known risk factors for ischaemic heart disease are age, male gender, smoking, hypertension and high serum total cholesterol levels (or a high ratio of low density lipoprotein to high density lipoprotein); other widely accepted risk factors include a diet rich in saturated fats and lack of exercise. Obviously the first two are not amenable to intervention. Not all those with these risk factors will develop coronary heart disease and many people who do not have the 'alterable' risk factors will subsequently develop the disease.

Reduction of these risk factors in an individual is believed to decrease his or her personal risk of developing ischaemic heart disease but we do not know what the intrinsic risk was to start with. At a population level we know that by reducing the prevalence of these risk factors in the community we can reduce the prevalence of the disease, but we are not sure by how much.

Screening for high blood pressure is important in this age group. Certainty of diagnosis requires repeated measurements of blood pressure over several weeks. Information on prevalence is likely to be most accurate from GP data as long as the GP takes the opportunity to measure the blood pressures of people who attend the surgery. This information would need to be collated and interpreted.

Systematic screening programmes may be in operation in some FHSAs or DHAs and make the process of collecting information easier. With the introduction of the new GP contract (1990) all new patients and people not seen by their GP for three years will be offered an examination at their GP's surgery which will measure blood pressure.

Health promotion clinics may screen for hypertension and be a source of information. Work medical examinations and occupational health examinations may also be a source of information on levels of hypertension.

(f) Menopausal problems

Sources of information on the nature and extent of problems thought to be associated with the menopause include:

- well woman centres/clinics;
- gynaecology outpatients;
- surveys of women;
- extrapolation from other surveys.

(g) Oral health

National surveys of the dental health of those aged from 45 to 54 years and from 55 to 64 years are available from the OPCS. They have been carried out every ten years since 1968. The General Household Survey also contains questions on dental health. Local data may be available from your local community dental service, particularly regarding adults with special needs. Some local community dental officers have carried out local surveys of edentulousness (proportion of people with no teeth).

3 MODIFIERS TO HEALTH EXPERIENCE

3.1 Socio-economic

Mortality from coronary heart disease shows a marked social class gradient, with much higher levels in deprived areas. The prevalence of avoidable risk factors, in particular smoking, is known to be higher in working-class communities but this probably only accounts for at most half of the increased mortality rate. It is believed by many that material deprivation and lack of social support contribute to the rest of the excess.

There is a very strong social class gradient in respiratory disease, probably because of the increased prevalence of smoking, increased atmospheric pollution at home and at work and poorer housing conditions, as well as the material deprivation mentioned above. There is a social class gradient in cancers except breast cancer and malignant melanoma (a form of skin cancer).

Sources of information
Social class, number in receipt of housing benefit, proportion of houses without basic amenities, housing tenure type and car ownership levels can all indicate areas of social deprivation. Composite scores include the Jarman and Townsend scores, which are available at ward level; the former will be available at practice level.

3.2 Environmental

(a) Urban versus rural

Respiratory disease is much more common in urban areas than in rural areas and in areas of heavy industry than in the suburbs, and is affected by climatic conditions. These effects are mediated through levels of atmospheric pollution, which markedly affect the prevalence of respiratory disease.

Sources of information
The local authority may record atmospheric pollution levels in the area.

(b)   Work

The work environment is a very important modifier of the health experience of this age group. Potential hazards to health at work include:

- accidents in heavy industry, farming and the construction industry;
- respiratory diseases in the mining industry;
- chemical- or radiation-induced cancers;
- stress associated with boring and repetitive jobs;
- repetitive strain injury in clerical staff;
- low back strain in labouring and nursing;
- lack of autonomy at work, which has been linked to the development of coronary heart disease;
- 'sick building' syndrome.

The work environment can also contribute to mental health problems (e.g. the strains of shift work).

Sources of information
Local knowledge of the main employers in your area can be obtained from the local office of the Department of Employment. Whether an employer in the local area is associated with known occupational hazards may be available from the occupational medicine department at your nearest medical school, the environmental health department of the local authority or from the public health medicine department of the health authority.

(c)   Housing

The housing type and standard may influence health experience at this life cycle stage. High-rise, deck access flats have been linked with poor mental health and high parasuicide and suicide rates, as well as increased rates of drug and alcohol misuse. Other adverse environmental conditions in the home include lack of basic amenities, damp conditions and overcrowding. A rare environmental hazard in the home may be radon gas.

Sources of information
The local authority housing department should have information on the types and standards of public sector housing as well as quality indicators, such as turnover of properties, percentage voids (empty properties) and waiting time for repairs. The proportion of houses lacking basic amenities and levels of overcrowding are available down to electoral ward level from census data. The proportion of public sector housing that is damp may be known to the housing department. Local surveys will be needed to assess the proportion of private houses suffering from damp conditions.

The environmental health department may have knowledge of the local situation regarding radon.

(d) Transport networks

Poor public sector transport systems will limit access to recreational activities and social support networks, as well as to health care facilities.

Sources of information
Local knowledge is important. The local authority and health authorities may have information on travelling times to services from various places in the district. Otherwise they will need to be calculated using information from the transport providers. Community transport groups and schemes such as 'dial-a-ride' may be able to provide information.

(e) Environmental hazards

As well as at work, people can be in contact with other environmental hazards in their daily lives. These include atmospheric carcinogens, radiation and water pollution.

Sources of information
The local authority, particularly the environmental health department, may have information about local environmental hazards.

3.3 Ethnic

Studies from the early 1970s showed that people born in different countries had different health experiences. Irish immigrants were at an increased risk of accidents, particularly work-related accidents, and of coronary heart disease. This latter increase is probably explained by a known higher prevalence of behaviourial risk factors, such as smoking and heavy drinking.

The same studies and others more recently have shown that Asians have a higher rate of coronary heart disease. This cannot be explained by an increased prevalence of known behaviourial risk factors as Asians are less likely to smoke and drink heavily. Some of the excess may be accounted for by a higher prevalence of diabetes. The effect of stress due to migration, racism and social isolation has been postulated as a reason for increased coronary heart disease rates, as has a diet high in fat. Genetic factors cannot be discounted.

Asians have been shown to have a low rate of cancer generally and an increased risk of tuberculosis; this latter is probably attributable to the reintroduction of tuberculosis to the UK by recent immigrants from Asia.

Afro-Caribbeans are known to be more likely to have high blood pressure, with a consequent increased likelihood of strokes. Other rare blood diseases (e.g. sickle cell anaemia) are more prevalent in areas with high Afro-Caribbean populations.

Sources of information
Census data provide information on the place of birth of the head of the household. This is routinely available at district and electoral ward level. This is not a true reflection of the ethnic minority population as it does not include those people from ethnic minority groups who were born in this country. The 1991 census should provide us with more accurate information on the ethnic composition of the local community as it asked a question on the self-perceived ethnic group membership of the members of the household.

Other qualitative information about the ethnic minority groups in your area (e.g. languages spoken, religion and country of origin) can be obtained from the Community Relations Council or from local representatives of the ethnic minority groups.

3.4 *Cultural*

Associated with social class and income differences, the local culture may in part affect beliefs and values about ill-health and the benefits of treatment, as well as the likelihood of people adopting healthy behaviours.

Sources of information
Anthropological and sociological studies would be needed to produce this information but local knowledge may hint at some of the issues.

4   HEALTH RESOURCES

Health resources potentially available to this age group include those listed below.

Within the individual
- self-esteem;
- education;
- awareness of risk and level of risk aversion;
- assertiveness;
- decision-making skills;
- communication skills.

Within the family
- family income;
- family support;

- communication within the family;
- willing and able carers for the sick and disabled.

Within the community
- community spirit;
- community support networks;
- church groups;
- availability of healthy work;
- pleasant environment to live in;
- neighbourliness.

Health service
Health education/promotion:
- coronary heart disease prevention programmes;
- cancer prevention programmes;
- osteoporosis prevention;
- community development.

Primary care and community health services:
- health promotion clinics;
- well woman centres;
- well man clinics;
- other screening clinics;
- cervical cytology service by GPs;
- cervical cytology service by DHA;
- self-help groups, e.g. smoking cessation, Look After Your Heart, anxiety and stress management;
- counselling services;
- community development workers;
- community physiotherapy;
- community dental service;
- community nursing;
- MacMillan nurses.

Secondary care:
- general medical/surgical services;
- gynaecology;
- cardiology/cardiac surgery;
- oncology (specialist cancer) services;
- rheumatology;
- orthopaedics;
- psychiatry;
- accident and emergency service;
- hospital dental services.

Local authority
Housing department:
- services for homeless people;
- provision of high quality public sector housing;

- relocation policies;
- policies for rehousing on medical grounds.

Education department:
- adult education courses.

Leisure services department:
- encouraging healthy exercise and recreation.

Transport services:
- community transport.

Social services:
- facilities for special needs groups.

Probation service
- alcohol education courses;
- drug education courses;
- life skills training;
- crime prevention initiatives.

Voluntary sector
- MacMillan nurses;
- community transport for disabled people;
- MIND;
- Samaritans;
- women's health groups;
- self-help groups for people with cancer;
- hospice provision;
- counselling services.

5   MODIFIERS TO USE OF SERVICES

5.1   Socio-economic

Working-class people have in the past been shown to be less likely to use preventive services, such as screening services. Whether this is because of a decreased perception of personal benefit or an increased perception of the cost of attending such services is not always clear. However, some services have managed to get a high attendance rate from working-class women (e.g. well woman centres). Lack of access to a car and lack of money for public transport costs mean that services are more likely to be used by this social group if they are local.

5.2   Environmental

Disabled people may not be able to use services that do not allow disabled access.

5.3 Ethnic

Asian women will need to be seen by a female doctor. Interpreters may be necessary for women whose first language is not English. Health education materials may need to be produced in languages other than English. If literacy rates are known to be low then videos or drama may be more appropriate ways of communicating.

6 SERVICE OPTIONS IN PRIMARY CARE

6.1 Health promotion in primary care

(a) Well woman centres/clinics

These are clinics that encourage women to take more control over their own and their family's health. They arose in response to the recognition that women are the main informal health educators in the community and that often their own personal health needs were not being met by a predominantly male run health service. They are not just health screening clinics (see Chapter 11).

(b) Well man clinics

These can be run with the same philosophy as well woman clinics but often they place more emphasis on pre-symptomatic screening and less on becoming an active participant in the health professional–patient relationship. In this age group screening for hypertension (high blood pressure) is valuable, particularly among Afro-Caribbean men. Advice on a healthy lifestyle is also appropriate. Although it is widely used, the general screening of blood cholesterol levels has not been found to be justifiable and should be restricted to those with a strong family history of coronary heart disease owing to high blood cholesterol levels.

(c) Smoking cessation groups

These can develop out of the well person clinics or independently of them. Some models have been found to be effective, particularly if a doctor is involved, but long-term follow up is required.

(d) Other health promotion clinics (e.g. Look After Your Heart)

These offer general advice in a supportive environment that aims to reduce the level of coronary heart disease risk factors and to encourage a healthy life-style, i.e. good diet, regular exercise, no smoking and a moderate alcohol intake.

(e) Coronary heart disease facilitators

Coronary heart disease facilitators are generally health professionals working in primary care teams to facilitate the organization of a health promotion and screening programme specifically to identify those at high risk of developing coronary (ischaemic) heart disease. It is important if a practice or the health authority employs a facilitator that he or she is well trained, not professionally isolated and works as part of the primary care team. He or she should work with clear, agreed protocols for screening services.

(f) Community development

Some people say that all the above attempts to improve the health of a community are inappropriate for those living in socially deprived areas. This is because they all depend on individuals recognizing that health is a priority in their life. For people on low incomes just surviving from day to day takes up the majority of their energy, time and money.

The community development approach focuses on working within the community's priorities and attempting to assist people in meeting what they perceive to be their immediate needs, including the requirements to improve their own and their family's health. These perceived needs of the community may differ from the health professional's defined need. In areas of social deprivation it may be appropriate for community development workers to be employed at practice or FHSA level.

(g) Cervical cytology

GPs and other primary care staff are well placed to carry out cervical cytology screening. Despite no longer using family planning services, women of this age remain fairly high users of primary care services and no opportunity should be missed to offer a woman who has never been screened a cervical cytology smear test. Recent research in the North West suggests that many women who die of cervical cancer have never been screened. A call and recall system is now in operation in all DHAs using the FHSA population register. This calls women to be screened every three or five years from age 20 until age 64.

In socially deprived areas the uptake may be very low, requiring much health promotion input to encourage women to attend, as well as needing a mobile, even domiciliary, service. In some areas a workplace screening service may be appropriate. However, local organizational changes may be all that are needed to 'flag' unscreened women for when they next visit the GP or primary care team.

Cervical cytology can be offered in screening clinics, health promotion clinics, well woman clinics, the workplace or the home. The practice nurse is often the person who takes the smear test.

(h)   Breast cancer screening

Breast cancer is by far the commonest cancer in this age group in women. It is a major cause of death and ill-health. Mammography has been shown to be capable of picking up very early stages of the disease, which it is believed will respond well to treatment. A screening service is now in operation for women between the ages of 50 and 64 years. This consists of inviting women for a mammogram every three years. Research suggests that a properly run screening service may reduce mortality by up to 30 per cent in women over 50 years of age.

The invitation to be screened has been shown to raise anxiety levels temporarily in many women. The role of the primary care team is to encourage women to respond to the invitation, to inform them about the reasons for and benefits of the service and to support them in coping with and resolving their anxiety.

6.2   Mental health

Options include:

- community psychiatric nurses attached to a practice to provide counselling and anxiety management programmes;
- counselling sessions;
- stress management courses;
- development of self-help groups by the primary care team.

6.3   Musculo-skeletal problems (problems with bones, joints and muscles)

The main role of primary care services is to provide easy access to community physiotherapy and, if necessary, specialist hospital services.

6.4   Accidents

An open access wound dressing service by GPs or practice nurses with referral to hospital or physiotherapy as appropriate.

REFERENCES

1 Martin, J., Meltzer, H. and Elliot, D. (1988) *The Prevalence of Disability among Adults*. OPCS Surveys of Disability in Great Britain Report 1. London: OPCS, HMSO.
2 Badley, E. M. and Tennant, A. (1988) *Calderdale Health and Disablement Survey*. Report from the Arthritis and Rheumatism Research Council Epidemiology Research Unit, University of Manchester.

13 / LIFE STAGE: FROM 65 TO 74 YEARS

1 INFLUENCES ON HEALTH

The death rate begins to rise dramatically at this life cycle stage, being nearly three times the rate of the previous decade. Deaths in this age group account for 30 per cent of male deaths and 20 per cent of female deaths. The death rate is nearly twice as high for men as for women.

As might be expected, the major causes of death and disability in both men and women are ischaemic (also called coronary) heart disease, cerebrovascular disease, cancers and respiratory disease, some of which are assumed to be preventable even at this age. The sex differences are mainly reflected in the proportionately higher burden of cancers and cerebrovascular disease (strokes) in women, but in absolute numbers more men die in every disease group than women.

GP consultation rates are substantially higher in this age range than in the previous age range of 45–64 years. The main reasons arise from heart disease and respiratory disease but there are also problems with muscles, bones and joints. All these disorders can and in many cases do lead to functional impairment and disability. Most people in this age group do lead an active and healthy existence but the prevalence of chronic (long-standing) disabling illness is high.

Studies have shown that 95 per cent of people over 65 years old live in the community rather than in institutions. Ninety per cent have been shown to be able to go about unassisted, although more than half have their activities restricted in some way. Many of these will be over 75 years old, however, and thus belong to the final life cycle stage.

In sociological parlance this is a time of changing social role, as most people in paid employment retire either before (many women retire at 60 years) or during this life cycle stage (some men retire at 60 years but most work until 65 years and a few beyond this age). There is a consequent need for adjustment.

Mortality

The major causes of death nationally are:

Males
1 Coronary heart disease.
2 Cancers.
3 Respiratory diseases.
4 Cerebrovascular diseases.
5 Digestive disorders.
6 Other heart diseases and lung circulation.
7 Nervous system diseases.
8 Endocrine (mainly diabetes).
9 Accidents and violence.
10 Mental disorders.

Females
1 Cancers.
2 Coronary heart disease.
3 Cerebrovascular diseases.
4 Respiratory diseases.
5 Digestive disorders.
6 Other heart diseases and lung circulation.
7 Endocrine (mainly diabetes).
8 Nervous system diseases.
9 Mental disorders.
10 Accidents and violence.

These ten causes account for 94 per cent of deaths in both men and women in this age group. The top four causes of death account for 84 per cent of deaths in men, with 65 per cent being caused by ischaemic heart disease and cancers alone. In women the top four account for just under 70 per cent of deaths. Cancers and ischaemic heart disease cause 33 and 27 per cent of deaths respectively.

The commonest sites for fatal cancers are:

Males
1 Lung.
2 Large bowel.
3 Prostate.
4 Stomach.
5 Leukaemias and lymphomas.

Females
1 Lung.
2 Breast.
3 Large bowel.
4 Leukaemias and lymphomas.
5 Ovary.

Morbidity

Consultation rates with GPs are very high in this age group, with three out of every four people consulting at least once during each year. Women consult slightly more than men but the excess is far less than in previous age bands. The only disease category for which there is a large difference in consultation rates is for mental disorders, in which women consult over twice as often as men. In absolute number terms (rather than rates) women consult about 30 per cent more as there are more women than men by this age group. The major reasons for consultation in 1981–2 were as follows.

Males
1 Circulatory diseases (includes coronary heart disease, strokes and heart failure).
2 Respiratory diseases.
3 Musculo-skeletal problems.
4 Ill-defined conditions.
5 Nervous system diseases.
6 Digestive disorders.
7 Skin diseases.
8 Accidents and violence.
9 Mental disorders.
10 Genito-urinary diseases.

Females
1 Circulatory diseases.
2 Musculo-skeletal problems.
3 Respiratory diseases.
4 Ill-defined conditions.
5 Nervous system diseases.
6 Mental disorders.

7 Accidents and violence.
8 Skin diseases.
9 Digestive disorders.
10 Genito-urinary diseases.

2 SOURCES OF INFORMATION ON HEALTH

2.1 Demography

The census provides data on the numbers of district and electoral ward residents in this age group. Annual projections are produced. Household composition is also available, giving numbers of lone pensioner households.

2.2 Mortality

Death rates for all causes, for each classification of death and for many individual causes are routinely available by age group, sex and district. They can also be produced at electoral ward level, although for some individual causes the numbers involved will be too small for meaningful comparisons (see Chapter 3).

Deaths from cancer are available from the local regional cancer registry. Your public health medicine department should be able to provide you with information from this. If information is postcoded it is in principle possible to produce statistics by DHA, FHSA or smaller areas. Again, for many rare cancers the small numbers involved could lead to misleading comparisons being made.

2.3 Morbidity

(a) General

Routine data sources include:

- the Körner Episode System (KES), which can provide information on hospital admissions in this age group – it must be remembered that hospital admission rates are as much a reflection of bed availability, referral rates and admission policies as an indicator of need;
- the Körner Aggregated Returns System (KARS), which will provide some information about users of health authority community services.

National GP consultation rates are available but they are from 1981–2 and thus out of date. More up-to-date and local data from GP practices would be very useful. This would need to be collected, collated and interpreted locally.

The General Household Survey is a national survey carried out annually. It can provide national data on the prevalence of long-standing illness and limiting long-standing illness, and the percentage of people with restricted activity in the past 14 days. The information is presented by age group but is only available for the national population.

(b) Disability

By this life cycle stage the population prevalence of a disease process is becoming a less important indicator of need for health or social services than the level of functional disability experienced by this group. Unfortunately this is very difficult to obtain. Measures of disability within a community include the following.

Extrapolation from other national and regional studies
Rates of disability within age groups are unlikely to alter much between districts, so one way to predict the prevalence of disability in your community is to extrapolate from national surveys. In 1988 the OPCS published the latest national survey of disability (cited in Chapter 12). This found that 283 per thousand people in the age group 60–74 years suffered some disability. The major types of disability were:

- locomotion or mobility problems in 195 per thousand;
- hearing loss in 108 per thousand;
- problems with personal care in 93 per thousand;
- dexterity problems in 76 per thousand;
- problems with vision in 52 per thousand.

A survey of the prevalence of disability in the community was carried out by the Arthritis Research Council in Calderdale in 1988 (cited in Chapter 12). The results of this survey showed that 272 of every thousand people in the 65–74 age group had some difficulties limiting their lives. Sixty-seven per thousand relied upon others in some areas of their lives and 34 per thousand were reliant on others for help with some daily activities, such as toileting, dressing and getting in and out of bed. Six per thousand could not be left alone because they were very confused or suffering from mental, nervous or emotional problems, with no other physical disabilities.

These rates were about twice those for the previous age group. The main causes of disability in the over-65 age group were found to be arthritis, heart disease, respiratory disorders, other soft tissue disorders, 'old age' and strokes.

Local data
A local community survey could be undertaken but this is likely to be expensive and time-consuming and is not likely to produce markedly

different results from other surveys. However, such a survey could be designed to obtain more information than just levels of disability. Advice on how to carry out such a survey can be obtained from your local public health medicine department.

Information can be obtained from GPs and primary care teams. GPs with an age–sex register should be able to 'flag' people in this age group and ask about their levels of disability, either opportunistically when they next attend the surgery or prospectively by sending out a questionnaire. However, questionnaires on disability must be validated first. Your public health medicine department should be able to advise you further.

Information may be obtained from the social services department of the local authority. The social services department should have a list of people in this age group in the area who are in receipt of their services. Good sources of information may be the home help or the domestic care organizers. It must be remembered that this information will be a reflection of *demand* or *met need* rather than of the true need for these services. The introduction of *case assessment* (or *management*) means that care managers should have much information on the social care needs of individuals referred to them. This will have to be collated and interpreted in order to be useful.

Information is obtainable from voluntary sector organizations. Certain organizations campaigning for or providing services for disabled people or the elderly may have local information on *known prevalence* of disability in the community. This is likely to underestimate the true prevalence. Examples of such organizations include Age Concern, community transport organizations and the Disabled Living Foundation. These organizations may also be able to provide more qualitative information about the experiences of disabled people in your community and about gaps they perceive in the services offered.

Information is obtainable from the local authority housing department. The housing department may have information on the numbers of requests and acceptances of medical reasons for rehousing in people in this age group. Many of these are for disabilities associated with daily living.

(c) Cancer

The number of people in each district health authority diagnosed as having cancer is available from the regional cancer registry. Incidence rates and prevalence ratios can be computed. See above under Mortality for details.

(d) Oral health

National surveys of the dental health of people aged 64–75 years are available from the OPCS. Surveys have been carried out by them every ten years since 1968. The General Household Survey also contains questions on dental health. Local data may be available from your community dental service, particularly regarding adults with special needs. Some community dental officers have done surveys of edentulousness (proportion of people with no teeth).

3 MODIFIERS TO HEALTH EXPERIENCE

3.1 Socio-economic

The social class gradient still exists in the major causes of death in this age group, but is less marked than in the younger age groups. If, as is often the case, retirement is associated with a substantial drop in income, this can lead to a poor diet and an inability to maintain and heat the house. All of these can lead to an increase in ill-health.

Sources of information
Social class, number in receipt of housing benefit, level of basic amenities, housing tenure type and car ownership levels can all indicate areas of social deprivation. Composite scores include the Jarman and Townsend scores which are available at ward level; the former will be available at practice level.

3.2 Environmental

(a) General environmental conditions

The level of atmospheric pollution affects the prevalence and severity of respiratory disease. Hence respiratory disease is commoner in urban than in rural environments and is affected by climatic conditions. Public water supply pollution or poor drinking water quality is another possible environmental hazard (e.g. high level of nitrates).

Sources of information
The local authority may have information on levels of atmospheric and water pollution. Some environmental pressure groups conduct studies on pollution.

(b) Work

As most people have retired by this age the work environment is not an important part of their exposure to environmental hazards. However, it should be recognized that exposure to such hazards can lead to ill-health at later stages in life, so the health of this age group is determined in many ways by exposure to environmental or behaviourial hazards in the past (see the discussion of cohort and period effects in Chapter 3).

Sources of information
Whether the major employers in the area are associated with particular environmental hazards may be known to the environmental health department.

(c)   Housing

Housing type and standard may influence the health of this age group even more than that of younger age groups. The rising prevalence of mobility problems makes the provision of appropriate housing very important. Inappropriate housing can lead to social isolation and consequent poor mental and physical health. Other adverse environmental conditions in the home include lack of basic amenities, damp conditions and overcrowding. A further rare environmental hazard in the home may be radon gas.

Sources of information
The local authority housing department should have information on the types and standard of public sector housing, including that provided especially for vulnerable elderly people. Quality indicators of public sector housing include turnover of properties, percentage of voids (empty properties) and waiting times for repairs. For information on the standard of private sector housing a local survey will probably be required. The environmental health department of the local authority may have knowledge of the local situation concerning levels of radon.

(d)   Transport networks

Good public sector transport systems are very important to the elderly, a smaller proportion of whom, compared to other adults, have access to a car and many of whom cannot walk far. Lack of good transport networks will limit access to recreational activities, social support networks and health service facilities.

Sources of information
Local knowledge is important. The local authority and health authorities may have information on travelling times to services from various places in the district. Otherwise they will need to be calculated using information from the transport providers. Community transport groups and schemes such as 'dial-a-ride' may be able to provide information.

(e)   Environmental hazards

As well as in the home people can be exposed to environmental hazards in their daily lives. These include particulate atmospheric pollution, radiation and water pollution.

Sources of information
The local authority's environmental health department may have information on local environmental hazards.

3.3 Ethnic

People of Afro-Caribbean origin have a higher risk of high blood pressure, with a consequent increase in the number of strokes. Asians have been found in general to have a higher risk of developing coronary heart disease and diabetes and a lower risk of developing cancer. The OPCS disability survey found that Afro-Caribbeans had a higher prevalence of disability than whites; Asians had a slightly lower prevalence of disability than whites.

Sources of information
Census data provide a breakdown of the place of birth of the head of household. This is routinely available at district and electoral ward level. The figures do not truly reflect the numbers from an ethnic minority group as they do not include the numbers of people born in this country who would still be considered a member of an ethnic group. This should be rectified by the 1991 census, which asked a question on self-perceived ethnic group membership. More qualitative information (e.g. language spoken, customs, religion, country of origin) may be obtained from the Community Relations Council or by speaking to representatives of the ethnic minority groups in the community.

3.4 Cultural

The experiences of ageing, such as bereavement, the death of close friends and peers, and a lack of understanding of and tolerance for youth culture, may lead to a kind of 'culture of old age' in which social isolation and low status are accepted. This can induce a tolerance of health impairment as *an unavoidable consequence of ageing* and in consequence reduce expectations that the impact of unavoidable impairments can be minimized. In this age group as in others the local culture may in part affect beliefs and values about ill-health and the benefits of treatment, as well as the likelihood of adopting healthy behaviours. Cultural differences may lead to differences in the social support available from younger members of the family.

Sources of information
Anthropological and sociological studies would be needed to produce this information but local knowledge may hint at some of the issues.

4 HEALTH RESOURCES

Health resources available to this group include the following.

Within the individual
- education;
- sense of autonomy;
- self-esteem;
- assertiveness;
- level of physical fitness;
- ability to relax.

Within the family
- family income;
- availability of willing and able carers;
- family support.

Within the community
- neighbourliness;
- support for carers;
- community spirit;
- social support networks;
- pleasant and stimulating environment to live in;
- disabled access to community buildings and areas.

Health service
Health education/promotion:
- community development;
- training to improve sense of self-esteem;
- coronary heart disease prevention;
- cancer prevention and early detection.

Primary care and community health services:
- health promotion clinics;
- screening service;
- well woman centres;
- well man clinics;
- cervical cytology service;
- community chiropody;
- community physiotherapy;
- community nursing;
- continence adviser;
- community dental service;
- MacMillan nurses;
- counselling service.

Secondary care:
- general medical/surgical services;
- oncology (specialist cancer) services;

- geriatric services (including day care);
- accident and emergency service;
- psychogeriatric service;
- psychiatric services;
- orthopaedic services;
- rheumatology;
- rehabilitation, including physiotherapy and occupational therapy;
- ophthalmology;
- respite care;
- hospice provision;
- ambulance service;
- hospital dental service.

Local authority
Housing department:
- provision of appropriate housing (including protection from intruders) for elderly people;
- appropriate system for rehousing on medical grounds;
- service for elderly homeless people;
- adaptations to the home.

Social services:
- home help/domestic care service;
- meals on wheels;
- community alarm networks;
- laundry service for incontinence sufferers;
- day centres;
- provision of aids for daily living;
- adaptations to the home;
- services for carers, e.g. respite care, night-sitting service etc;
- institutional care, e.g. elderly persons' homes.

Education department:
- adult education classes.

Leisure services department:
- appropriate leisure facilities that encourage exercise and recreation.

Transport services department:
- community transport provision.

Probation service and police
Crime prevention initiatives to allay the fears of elderly people concerning the possibility of being attacked (particularly in their homes).

Voluntary sector
Options include:
- MacMillan nurses;
- community transport;

- hospice provision;
- lunch clubs;
- day centres;
- residential care;
- nursing homes;
- counselling services.

Private sector
Options include:
- residential care;
- nursing homes;
- domestic care service;
- transport services;
- leisure facilities;
- health screening.

5 MODIFIERS TO USE OF SERVICES

5.1 Socio-economic

Poor mobility, lack of access to a car and poor public transport networks make it much more of a burden to use any health service facilities not provided in the home. Money can compensate to some extent by enabling the use of taxis or giving access to a car. Lower levels of disposable income therefore reduce access to services not provided in the home.

Working-class people have in the past been shown to be less likely to use preventive services, such as screening services. Whether this is because of a decreased perception of personal benefit or an increased perception of the cost of attending such services is not always clear. Many local services, domiciliary services and appropriate services do manage to get high uptake rates from working-class people.

5.2 Environmental

Access is restricted to all services if there is no provision for the disabled (e.g. lack of ramps and lifts).

5.3 Ethnic

Elderly people from ethnic minority groups are less likely than younger people to be able to speak English confidently, and therefore there is a need for interpreters and written information in languages other than English. As at other life cycle stages, Asian women will need to be seen by female doctors (and other health professionals) if they have to undress or require an internal examination.

5.4 Cultural

Research has shown that older people use services less frequently than the young because they have poor expectations of their health and in some cases because of a desire not to be a trouble to health care professionals.

6 SERVICE OPTIONS IN PRIMARY CARE

6.1 Health promotion and disability prevention

(a) Domiciliary elderly screening service, particularly to pick up:
   - high blood pressure;
   - poor vision;
   - hearing loss;
   - depression;
   - dementia;
   - Parkinson's disease;
   - incontinence;
   - poor oral health and ill-fitting dentures;
   - diabetes;
   - anaemia;

   with a system of treatment or referral as appropriate, and follow-up.
(b) Chiropody service – domiciliary and surgery based.
(c) Easy access to community physiotherapist.
(d) Easy access to community occupational therapist.
(e) Continence adviser.
(f) Cervical cytology service: It remains important to screen for cervical disorders those who have never been screened in this age group. The present call and recall service only calls people until the age of 64 years. Opportunistic screening, a local call and recall service and a domiciliary service may be needed.
(g) District nursing service.
(h) Provision of aids and appliances.

6.2 Mental health service

(a) Bereavement and other counselling service — domiciliary and surgery based.
(b) Stress management courses.
(c) Service for people with dementia:
   - assessment and follow-up by primary health care team staff;
   - self-help groups for carers;
   - professional support for carers.

6.3 *Liaison between primary health care and social services*

(a) Social worker or care manager attached to primary care team.
(b) Joint assessment of health and social care needs.
(c) Benefit advice, e.g. disabled living allowance, disabled work allowance, attendance allowance, invalid care allowance and community charge (and subsequently council tax) rebates.
(d) Aids and appliances store.

LIFE STAGE:
75 YEARS AND OVER

1 INFLUENCES ON HEALTH

Forty-four per cent of male deaths and 64 per cent of female deaths occur over 74 years of age. The causes of death are broadly similar between men and women, although cerebrovascular disease is more frequent in women and breast cancer is the commonest cancer in women. Over this age women greatly outnumber men and the absolute number of deaths in women is greater than in men. Women outnumber men by two to one over 74 years and by over three to one over 84 years.

As everyone eventually dies of something death rates in this age group are a particularly poor measure of health in a community, although some years of extra life could theoretically be saved. The aim of the health service in this life cycle stage is to improve or maintain the quality of life as well as ensuring that where possible death is pain-free and dignified. This means that morbidity and disability measures are much more important than death rates. The major causes of death are given here simply as a proxy of morbidity, as one has to be ill with something before one dies of it.

There is evidence that death certificates are less accurate in this age group; elderly people often die with multiple pathologies (more than one condition at a time) and it is not always clear which of the pathologies are the immediate cause of death, underlying causes or merely incidental to death. As a consequence of multiple pathology older people frequently have low expectations of health and as a consequence often have unmet health needs.

A study on the elderly in the Scottish borders revealed that only 7 per cent were free from any surveyed medical condition; 60 per cent had three or more different conditions; 70 per cent had at least one condition unknown to their GP but that nevertheless had a significant impact on their lives.

Mortality

The major causes of mortality nationally in this age group are as follows.

Males
1 Coronary heart disease.
2 Cancers.
3 Respiratory diseases.
4 Cerebrovascular disease.
5 Other heart diseases.
6 Other arterial disease.
7 Digestive disorders.
8 Mental disorders.
9 Genito-urinary diseases.
10 Accidents (falls account for 50 per cent).

Females
1 Coronary heart disease.
2 Cerebrovascular disease.
3 Cancers.
4 Respiratory diseases.
5 Other heart diseases.
6 Mental disorders.
7 Digestive disorders.
8 Other arterial disease.
9 Genito-urinary diseases.
10 Accidents (falls account for 68 per cent).

The above cause 85 per cent of deaths in males and 90 per cent of deaths in females in this age group.

The commonest fatal cancer sites nationally are as follows.

Males
1 Lung.
2 Prostate.
3 Stomach.

4 Unspecified.
5 Large bowel.

Females
1 Breast.
2 Lung.
3 Large bowel.
4 Stomach.
5 Lymphatic system.

Morbidity

(a)   GP consultations

Over three-quarters of people in this age group have a consultation with their GP each year. Women consult more often than men. Circulatory diseases, respiratory diseases, and bone, joint and muscle problems (musculo-skeletal) predominate. The major reasons for consultation in a national study in 1981–2 were as follows.

Males
1 Circulatory diseases (includes coronary heart disease, strokes and heart failure).
2 Respiratory diseases.
3 Ill-defined conditions.
4 Musculo-skeletal problems.
5 Nervous system diseases.
6 Digestive system diseases.
7 Skin diseases.
8 Accidents and violence.
9 Mental disorders.
10 Genito-urinary disorders.

Females
1 Circulatory diseases.
2 Ill-defined conditions.
3 Musculo-skeletal problems.
4 Respiratory diseases.
5 Nervous system diseases.
6 Mental disorders.
7 Accidents and violence.
8 Digestive system diseases.
9 Skin diseases.
10 Genito-urinary disorders.

(b) Physical disability

In this age group the prevalence of the disease process is less an indicator of need for health and social services than is the resulting disability and reduction in the quality of life.

The OPCS national survey of the prevalence of disability in 1988 (cited in Chapter 12) estimated that overall 533 per thousand men over 75 years of age had some disability and 631 per thousand women. The prevalence was higher at older age groups, with 466 per thousand men and women aged 75–79 and 779 per thousand over 85 years of age. The main areas of disability were locomotion, hearing, personal care, vision and dexterity.

A community study by the Arthritis Research Council in Calderdale in 1988 (cited in Chapter 12) found that 483 per thousand population over 75 years of age had some disability, with 228 per thousand being in some way dependent on others and 82 per thousand dependent on others for important daily activities, such as dressing, toileting or getting into and out of bed. The commonest reasons for disability in this study in this age group were 'old age', hearing loss, vision loss, nervous and psychological disorders, neurological disorders and joint and bone problems.

(c)   Mental disability

Senile dementia is an important problem in this age group. The amount of undetected mental illness makes it essential actively to seek out cases if an accurate assessment of prevalence is to be made.

Dementia is of two main types: Alzheimer type and multi-infarct dementia. The cause of the former is badly understood. The latter accounts for 30 per cent of cases and is caused by a series of small strokes, some of which may be preventable by reductions in levels of high blood pressure in the younger age groups.

Fifteen per cent of the over-75 group and 20 per cent of the over-85 group suffer from dementia. In an average GP practice one in ten people over 65 will be suffering from dementia. Studies have found that between 80 and 90 per cent of cases of dementia are unknown to their family doctors.

Dementia is not the only mental health problem in old age. Many more elderly people suffer from depression than dementia. Community surveys suggest that about 17 per cent of people over 65 are depressed. The prevalences are twice as high for women (23 per cent) as for men (12 per cent). Physical illness and bereavement may be the causes of this high level of depression.

2 SOURCES OF INFORMATION ON HEALTH

2.1 Demography

The census provides data on the numbers of district and electoral ward residents in this age group. Household composition is available to give the numbers of lone pensioner households. The proportion of the elderly population in private households compared with the proportion in other establishments can also be determined.

2.2 Mortality

Death rates for all causes, for each classification of disease and for many individual causes are routinely available by age group, sex and district. These are not particularly useful in this age group.

Deaths from cancer are available from the local regional cancer registry. Your local public health medicine department will be able to give you the address. If the registry information is postcoded it is theoretically possible to produce statistics by FHSA and smaller areas. For many rare cancers the small numbers involved could lead to misleading comparisons.

2.3 Morbidity

(a) General

Routine data sources include:

- the Körner Episode System (KES), which can provide diagnoses and other hospital admission information in this age group – it must be remembered, however, that hospital admission rates are as much a reflection of bed availability, referral rates and admission policies as an indicator of need;
- the Körner Aggregated Returns System (KARS), which will provide some information about users of health authority community services.

National GP consultation rates are available but they are now out of date. More up-to-date and local information would be useful. This would need to be collected, collated and interpreted locally.

The General Household Survey is a national survey carried out annually. It can provide national data on the prevalence of long-standing illness and limiting long-standing illness, and the percentage of people with restricted activity in the past 14 days. The information is available by age group but is only presented nationally.

(b) Physical and mental disability

Unfortunately, measures of disability within a community are hard to obtain. They include the following.

Extrapolation from national and regional studies
The two studies mentioned above can be used to work out the expected numbers and types of disability within this age group in your own local population.

Local data
A local community survey could be undertaken but this is likely to be time-consuming and expensive, and is unlikely to produce markedly different results from the OPCS and Calderdale studies. However, it could be widened to provide other information. Advice on how to carry out such a study can be obtained from your public health medicine department.

The new GP contract requires that GPs or members of the primary health care team offer an annual screening service to people over 75 years of age on their practice list. If a system can be devised whereby this information can be collated and analysed then it will provide very useful data for health and social care planners and for providers on the prevalence of disability and consequent health and social care needs of the local elderly population. Advice on how to go about setting up such a system can be obtained from the local public health medicine department.

From 1993 social services departments will carry out care assessments of all people referred to them. If this information can be collated then it will be invaluable for health needs assessors. Other good sources of information might be home help or domestic care organizers. It must be remembered, however, that this information will be a reflection of *demand* or *met need* rather than of true need for these services.

Certain voluntary sector organizations campaigning for disabled people or the elderly may have local information on known prevalence of disability in the community. This is unlikely to reflect the true prevalence. Examples of such organizations include Age Concern, community transport organizations and Help the Aged. There may be voluntary sector nursing or residential homes in the area, which would be able to provide information on the levels of disability and consequent health care needs of their residents.

The housing department may have information on the number of requests for and acceptances of medical rehousing in people in this age group. Many of these are for disabilities associated with daily living. The local authority may also provide sheltered accommodation for elderly people and would have information on these residents.

Hospital admission data will be available from geriatric, psychiatric, psychogeriatric and ESMI (elderly severely mentally ill) units.

(c) Cancer

The number of people in each DHA or FHSA diagnosed as having cancer is available from the local regional cancer registry. For further details see under Mortality above.

(d) Oral health

National surveys of the dental health of people aged over 75 years are available from the OPCS. Surveys have been carried out by them every ten years since 1968. The General Household Survey also contains questions on dental health. Local data may be available from your community dental service, which provides a dental service to vulnerable groups. In some areas this includes the elderly. Some community dental officers have done surveys of edentulousness (proportion of people with no teeth).

3   MODIFIERS TO HEALTH EXPERIENCE

3.1   Socio-economic

Old age has been termed the 'great leveller'. In some ways this is true, but the quality of life of an elderly person has still been shown to be affected by the amount of disposable income. Poverty is common in the elderly from any social class background but it is more common among those from a working-class background.

Poverty leads to an inability to heat and maintain the house, a poor diet and less access to appropriate private transport to maintain social networks. All of these can lead to increased ill-health. Other social indicators known to increase the risk of ill health in the elderly include:

- living in isolation;
- being newly widowed;
- being housebound;
- being recently discharged from hospital;
- having recently moved to sheltered accommodation.

Sources of information
Occupational social class is not a useful marker at this life cycle stage. The number of pensioners in receipt of housing benefit, housing tenure and type, and levels of car ownership are less useful measures of poverty and social deprivation in this age group than in younger age groups.

Composite scores of social deprivation in an area include the Jarman and Townsend scores, which are available at electoral ward level; the former will also be available at practice level. To measure levels of social isolation, recent bereavement and the number housebound would require a special community survey.

3.2 Environmental

(a) General conditions

The major environmental modifier to disease in this age group is the cold, both within the home and outside it. There are many more deaths in winter than in summer.

(b) Housing

Housing type and standard influence the health of this group through people's ability to maintain an appropriate ambient temperature. Large, poorly insulated, poorly maintained houses are likely to be cold. The home environment will also influence mobility and the risk of accidents and falls. Inappropriate housing can increase the effects of poor mobility, such as social isolation and a poor diet. Other adverse environmental conditions in the home include dampness, which increases respiratory diseases, and lack of basic amenities. Poor lighting in the house will increase visual disability.

Sources of information
The local authority housing department should have local information on the types and standards of public sector housing, including that provided especially for the elderly. For information on the standard of private sector housing a local survey would probably be needed.

(c) Transport networks

Good public sector transport systems are very important in the elderly, a very small proportion of whom have access to private transport. Lack of good transport networks will limit access to recreational activities, social support networks and health service facilities.

Sources of information
Local knowledge is important here. The local authority and health authority may have information on travelling times from various parts of the district to major health and social service facilities. Otherwise the information would have to be assembled from information obtained from the transport providers. Community transport organizations may have some useful information.

3.3 Ethnic

The OPCS disability study found that Afro-Caribbean people had a higher prevalence of disability than whites, with Asians having a slightly lower rate. The high rate among Afro-Caribbean people may be a reflection of the increased prevalence of hypertension, and hence strokes. Asians have overall been found to have a higher risk of coronary heart disease and a lower risk of cancer. Diabetes is particularly prevalent among Asians.

Sources of information
Census data provide a breakdown of the place of birth of the head of household. This is routinely available at district and electoral ward level. This information does not, however, truly reflect the numbers from an ethnic minority group as it does not include the numbers of people born in this country who would still consider themselves a member of an ethnic group. The 1991 census should be more helpful in this respect. Other more qualitative information on religion, country of origin, languages spoken and customs can be obtained by talking to the Community Relations Council or to representatives of the local ethnic community.

3.4 Cultural

In some cultures the elderly are revered for their wisdom and experience. In our society we tend to consider old people a burden on society and accord them low status. The experiences of ageing, such as bereavement, the death of close friends and peers, and a lack of understanding of and tolerance for the youth culture, may lead to a kind of 'culture of old age' in which social isolation and low status are accepted. This may lead to a tolerance of health impairment as an unavoidable consequence of ageing rather than as something whose impact can be minimized.

In this age group as in others the local culture may in part affect beliefs and values about ill-health and the benefits of treatment, as well as the likelihood of adopting healthy behaviours.

Cultural differences may lead to differences in the social support available from younger members of the family. However, there is little evidence that the elderly in this country are not cared for by their relatives. Where it is geographically and economically possible most relatives do support their elderly kin. Health is likely to be better in those who are receiving support from relatives.

Sources of information
The census data provide a breakdown of the number of households in which an elderly person is living but is not head of the household. Anthropological and sociological studies and community surveys may provide very useful information on local beliefs in this age group.

4 HEALTH RESOURCES

Health resources available to this group include the following.

Within the individual
- expectations of health and non-acceptance of poor health;
- sense of self-worth;
- education.

Within the family
- family income;
- availability of willing and able carers;
- sense of value of elderly relatives;
- family support.

Within the community
- neighbourly support;
- community spirit;
- support for carers;
- pleasant and stimulating environment to live in;
- ease of access for disabled people to community areas.

Health service
Health education/promotion:
- community development;
- disability prevention and amelioration;
- advice on diet and keeping warm;
- early detection of cancer.

Primary care and community health services:
- elderly screening service;
- well woman centres;
- well man clinics;
- community chiropody;
- community physiotherapy;
- community nursing;
- counselling service;
- community dental service;
- MacMillan nurses.

Secondary care:
- general medical/surgical services;
- geriatric service, including day hospital;
- psychogeriatric service;
- ESMI (elderly severely mentally infirm) service;
- psychiatric service;
- orthopaedic service;
- rheumatology;

- rehabilitation service, including physiotherapy and occupational therapy;
- accident and emergency service;
- ophthalmology;
- respite care;
- hospice provision;
- hospital dental service.

Local authority
Housing department:
- provision of appropriate housing for elderly people;
- appropriate system of rehousing on medical grounds;
- service for elderly homeless people;
- system to adapt homes for disabled people;

Social services department:
- home help/domestic care service;
- meals on wheels;
- community alarms;
- laundry service for incontinence sufferers;
- day centres;
- provision of aids and appliances;
- services for carers, e.g. respite care, day- and night-sitting services;
- institutional care, e.g. elderly persons' homes.

Leisure services department:
- appropriate leisure services that encourage exercise, recreation and social networks.

Transport services department:
- community transport provision.

Probation service and police
Crime prevention initiatives are important. Many elderly people express fear of being attacked, particularly in their homes.

Voluntary sector
Services include:
- day centres;
- residential care;
- nursing homes;
- lunch clubs;
- social clubs;
- hospice provision;
- bereavement counselling;
- counselling;
- community transport;
- MacMillan nurses;
- advice centres;

- befriending services;
- complementary therapists.

Private sector
Services include:
- residential care;
- nursing homes;
- domestic care;
- transport services;
- leisure facilities;
- complementary therapists;
- health screening.

5   MODIFIERS TO USE OF SERVICES

5.1   Socio-economic

Poor mobility, lack of access to a car and poor public transport networks make it much more of a burden and often an impossibility to make use of any health service facilities not provided in the home. Money can compensate to some extent by allowing the use of taxis or by giving access to a car. People with less disposable income are therefore at a disadvantage.

Working-class people have in the past been shown to be less likely to use preventive services.

5.2   Ethnic

Elderly people from ethnic groups are particularly likely to have problems with English as their second language and there is therefore a need for interpreters and written information in languages other than English. Literacy can also be a problem, so using videos or drama may be a better way to relate health information. Asian women will need to be seen by a woman doctor or other health service professional if there is a requirement to undress or undergo an internal examination.

5.3   Cultural

Elderly people have been shown to underestimate their health care needs, to have low expectations of health and not to use health services as much as the younger age groups given their high levels of ill-health. Part of the reason for this is a concern not to be a burden on health service staff.

6 SERVICE OPTIONS IN PRIMARY CARE

6.1 Health promotion and disability prevention

(a) Domiciliary elderly screening service, particularly to pick up:
   - high blood pressure;
   - poor vision;
   - hearing loss;
   - depression;
   - dementia;
   - Parkinson's disease;
   - incontinence;
   - poor oral health and ill-fitting dentures;
   - diabetes;
   - anaemia;

   with a system of treatment or referral as appropriate, and follow-up.
(b) Chiropody service – domiciliary and surgery based.
(c) Easy access to a community physiotherapist.
(d) Easy access to a community occupational therapist.
(e) Continence adviser.
(f) District nursing.

6.2 Mental health service

(a) Bereavement and other counselling service – domiciliary and surgery based.
(b) Assessment and follow-up of people with dementia.
(c) Support for carers – professional and self-help.

6.3 Liaison between primary health care and social services

(a) Social worker or care manager attached to the primary care team.
(b) Joint assessment of health and social care needs.
(c) Benefit advice, e.g. mobility allowance, attendance allowance, invalid care allowance, poll tax rebates.
(d) Aids and appliances store.

6.4 Terminal/palliative care

(a) Provision of 24-hour care from GPs and community nursing to allow terminally ill patients to be cared for at home.
(b) Access to complementary therapists employed through the ancillary staff budget.
(c) Support groups for terminally ill people, their families and their professional carers.
(d) Access to aids to improve quality of life.

15 / THE CHALLENGE OF PURCHASING FOR HEALTH GAIN

For the reformed NHS to function as intended there must be both dialogue and tension between purchasers and providers. Providers will set out their stalls and purchasers will seek to negotiate contracts that are advantageous, in terms of quality and cost, to their resident populations. It should be clear that even in conception the NHS market cannot be the economists' perfect market. There exist circumstances where a single purchaser will dominate (monopsony) and where a single provider will dominate (monopoly).

The providers are, in some respects, doing much as they always have. The main difference post-1991 is that they have to be more business-aware: they must have detailed accounting; they must deliver on contracts; they must encourage only clinical developments they can sell. In other respects, however, their role is much enhanced (see later). Notwithstanding this it is the purchasers who, in theory, will shape the future of the NHS. For it is they who must decide how to distribute their fixed resource on behalf of their resident populations. In practice they suffer two constraints: (a) NHS inertia; (b) their own competence.

The current pattern of services has evolved through the history of the NHS. This hospital-oriented, acute care and high-technology dominated service has arisen in response to professional and consumer demand and has in turn fuelled those demands. To change this into a service with greater emphasis on health promotion, disease prevention, community-oriented care and the needs of the chronically ill will not be easy unless new resources become available. In any complex organization it is not possible suddenly to change the use of investments in plant and human resources. Even with new resources it would be hard to claw them from the insatiable appetite of existing services. Premature babies in neonatal intensive care, even though they are being treated to the point of diminishing returns, are far more appealing to the popular (and professional) imagination than the health, but mainly social, measures that might improve the quality of many pregnancies.

Any diversion of existing resources, or use of new resources, entails an opportunity cost: the 'cost', financial or otherwise, of not having used the money in some other way. The NHS has never been very good at considering opportunity cost but present circumstances bring this concept to the fore. The natural inertia of the NHS tends to support the notion of 'For whosoever hath, to him shall be given, and he shall have abundance; but whosoever hath not, from him shall be taken away even that which he hath' (Matthew 13: 12). Powerful professional and patient interest groups always do well.

Thus, purchasers can expect only to do the following.

1 Keep a firm grip on the introduction of service innovations, particularly those with large financial implications; many pharmaceutical products being marketed at present, or on the horizon, fall into this category. It should be borne in mind that innovation of itself need not be a bad thing: it may extend the range of medical competence; it may result in more cost-effective ways of achieving current aims. However, innovation should be accepted only if one's eyes are fully open to its likely consequences (direct cost, hidden consequential cost, opportunity cost and, most often forgotten, the health outcome).
2 Question the organization of some major existing services with a view to making them more responsive and effective in dealing with consumer needs. For example, it might be desirable to support the current trend of diverting much of the routine care of diabetics from hospital outpatient departments to community clinics.
3 Question, and perhaps seek to restrict, the use of some existing procedures of unproven benefit. For example, costly scanning techniques should be employed only in circumstances where there is a priori a good reason to believe that the findings will significantly inform diagnosis, treatment and prognosis; thus, there should be written clinical protocols guiding their use, and adherence to these should be monitored.
4 Identify and prioritize areas of unmet need to which some resource might be diverted. These will lie on the margin of existing service provision. And, as suggested in Chapter 2, the development of

primary care services and collaboration with non-NHS state sectors may prove a useful path to meeting such needs.

In the longer term, however, the cultural change in the NHS brought about by the introduction of strategic management could lead to greater changes and to the development of a health service which supports the care that is already going on in families and the community as well as providing appropriate secondary care.

Whereas providers have to acquire a few well defined skills, purchasers are charting largely unknown territory. The functions of purchasing are the assessment of health need, assembling health resource options to meet those needs, choosing among these options, translating them into contracts for health services and managing the non-contracting agenda. We shall not discuss the technicalities of negotiating and monitoring contracts, for these tasks *are* reasonably well defined and can easily be learned by those charged with them. Health needs assessment, the assembly of service options to meet needs and the appraisal of options are different matters.

Many public health physicians and some planners would assert that health needs assessment, option assembly and option appraisal have been practised for years. In a sense this is true, but we suggest that they have not taken place in a coherent manner and that the decision-making machinery of the pre-reformation NHS was incapable of effectively using the information that flowed from these exercises. They were symbolic, rather than substantive, acts (see the discussion in Chapter 12 of St Leger et al.[1]). Symbolic tasks do not command much resource; hence the impoverished nature of many routine NHS information systems and the paucity of useful information, routine or otherwise, about health need.

The challenge in health needs assessment and option appraisal is to use the resources now directed towards them in an effective manner. Providers are going to become increasingly business-like. If the purchasers do not take the reins the providers could run rings around them. The NHS will continue to muddle along to many people's satisfaction but opportunities to ensure that the service is effective, efficient, equitable and appropriate to the needs of the local population may be lost.

A MODEL FOR PURCHASING

There are five key elements to purchasing. These are health needs assessment, health resource option appraisal, prioritization, contracting and managing the non-contracting agenda. Influencing the resources of other organizations with whom we have no contract in order to meet need is an important aspect of improving public health. We include this in the term 'purchasing' here but it is sometimes referred to as commissioning.

Figure 15.1 displays a schematic view of the key purchasing activities. The upper left quadrant of the figure refers to health needs assessment. The lower left quadrant shows the assembly of resource options to meet needs and it should be noted that these include potential actions by other organizations, such as the city council and voluntary bodies. The lower right quadrant portrays option appraisal and prioritization. It should be noted that it is explicitly stated that actions are prioritized for marginal changes (be they changes to existing services or the development of new services on the margin). The upper right quadrant shows contracting and contract monitoring.

In this view the activities are cyclic and the development of services is mainly step-wise. The nature and the pace of work of a purchasing organization are determined by: the finance cycle (annual); the contracting cycle (this may vary for differing kinds of service); demands from the centre (unpredictable); and proposals for service developments emanating from providers. Clearly, to meet these exigencies it will be necessary to plan the use of the purchasing organization's own internal resources. That is, priorities are required within some policy framework.

POLICIES AND CRITERIA

In principle there should be an overall goal for the organization – a mission statement. This should make explicit what is hoped to be achieved with regard to health. It might be fairly nebulous and idealistic; more detailed aims and objectives could detail how the goal is to be achieved. Possibilities include:

- reduction of unacceptable variations in health (inequity), perhaps within the context of Health for All 2000;
- maximization of health potential;
- increasing population health overall;
- equity in the use of resources.

The first three are all examples of *health gain*. The four need not be incompatible if it is accepted that each places constraints on the optimization of the others.

Some might consider it best to use a vague and inoffensive slogan and to respond pragmatically to exhortations from the centre, such as those in *The Health of the Nation*.[2] However, Health for All does have an advantage in that the UK, alongside other nations, has adopted it in principle.

In practice the professionals engaged in health needs assessment might be expected to ascertain the problems on their 'patch' and justify their recommendations for action. It is in this context that checklists, of questions to ask before judging the merits of a case, are particularly helpful.

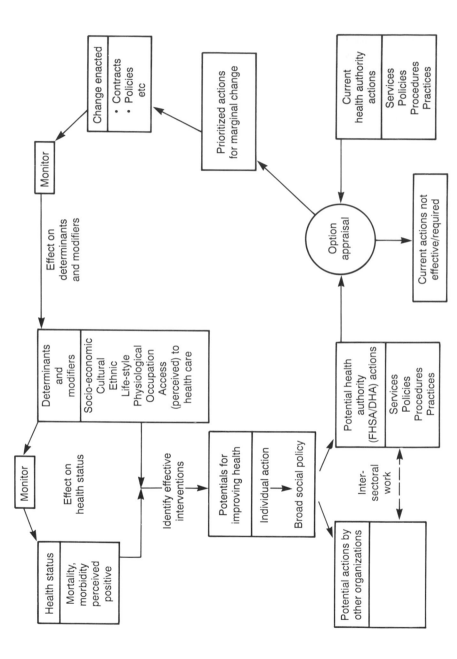

Figure 15.1 A schematic view of purchasing (after Unwin and Mercer[3])

It is possible to construct checklists that are reasonably value-free (or at least acceptable in a number of value systems) and that allow decisions to be made and judged openly. The checklists introduced below are intended to indicate the questions that might be asked. No attempt is made to suggest how the answers should be combined when forming a decision.

Appendix 1 lists questions to assist in judging whether substantial resources should be committed for the *detailed assessment* of what has been identified as a potential area of unmet health need. Appendix 2 lists issues to consider when considering whether or not to challenge the existence or manner of provision of a currently offered service. Similar checklists may be used when evaluating proposed service innovations.[4]

BRINGING ABOUT CHANGE

As mentioned in Chapter 2, health needs assessment is of no value unless it is used to inform decision-making within the purchasing organizations – both the DHA and FHSA. The decision to choose the priority areas for health needs assessment will be informed by:

- priorities from NHS Management Executive and the RHA;
- general policy considerations;
- resource availability;
- criteria such as those in Appendix 1.

When the area for detailed health needs assessment has been determined there are several steps to the practical process of health needs assessment (see Figure 15.2).

The first step is to define the problem. This falls into two parts. First, there must be an understanding of the nature of the need being addressed. This requires the clear definition of terms and an exploration of up-to-date knowledge. The published literature will be a valuable source but initially it can be easier to gain a view of the field by consulting experts. It should be borne in mind, however, that experts sometimes have a narrow perspective. At the completion of this stage one should have gained broad insight to the epidemiological, clinical and social dimensions of the problem. Moreover, it should be clear how the problem might be viewed in the life cycle context. The second aspect to defining the problem is to particularize it to the population under scrutiny. This is where the life cycle framework should be helpful in directing the search for information and imposing structure on the findings. The result of these exercises should be a profile of the problem, which, as far as practicable, should include:

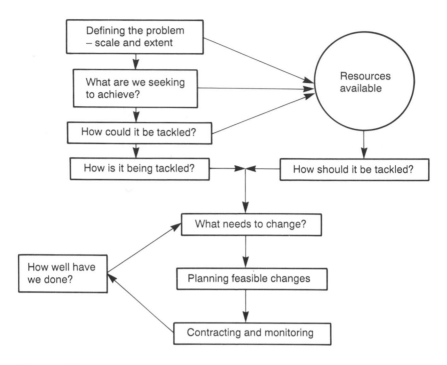

Figure 15.2 A schema for service development

- quantifying its extent;
- an indication of whether it is changing with time;
- a broad comparison with other places;
- identification of modifiers of particular relevance to the population at hand.

The second step is to agree what it is you are trying to achieve in health and quality outcome terms. This step needs to include both a professional and a public perspective. The latter can be obtained by using qualitative research techniques (see Chapter 4).

The third step is to consider what resources could be made available to address the identified need. This entails finding out about potential resources within the individual, the family, the community and the formal care services that could theoretically address the identified need. This book can help with this process. These considerations are theoretical or ideal; they need not be constrained by current patterns of service or by issues of financial resource. They set a standard against which the compromises of reality can be juxtaposed. For acute care, health technology assessment will be an important ingredient of this task, for only health resources of likely worth should be considered.

When considering the ideal it may be prudent to go beyond firm existing knowledge and practice to explore options currently under evaluation or on the more distant horizon, i.e. to indulge in futurology. When, later, one comes to propose changes practicable now, one should bear in mind the possibility that innovation may render obsolete much of the current and proposed investment in a service. For instance, islet cell transplantation might become universal and thus revolutionize the treatment of diabetes mellitus, or a vaccination may become available for the prevention of AIDS.

The fourth step is to gain a clear understanding of how the need is being met at present for the population under scrutiny. This entails a description of the configuration of the services (from any agency) meeting the need, the extent to which they meet it, their efficiency and their cost.

The fifth step will be carried out in collaboration with provider managers or clinicians. It entails designing a desirable and practicable service configuration that will meet the desired outcomes *within resource constraints*. This will be informed by the ideal identified during the second step and by the resources likely to be available. A number of options of differing resource requirements could be explored.

The sixth step is to juxtapose the conclusions from the third and fourth steps. This identifies the gap between current practice and planned practice, i.e. it asks 'what needs to change?' The changes must be identified, prioritized and approximately costed before final negotiations with potential providers are begun.

Given NHS inertia and its consequence that most changes will be at the margin, it is unlikely that major new services will come into being in one step or that existing services will be re-configured instantly. Thus, the process includes an assessment of progress and a feedback to the question about what needs to change. This is distinct from routine contract monitoring; it is a recognition that change will be iterative.

THE NON-CONTRACTING AGENDA

Health needs assessment, if carried out in the way we describe, will highlight health benefits that could be achieved if other agencies changed their ways of working or their resource distribution. Influencing other agencies is an important role for public health practitioners. The health needs assessment process gives direction and focus to multi-sectoral work.

The processes outlined in this and the previous sections are complicated, time-consuming and costly; hence our stricture above that health needs assessment and the other tasks of purchasing should take place within a policy framework directing the use of these investigative and planning resources. However, the task will be greatly simplified by the sharing of information between purchasing organizations and by collaboration with providers.

SHARING AND COLLABORATION

Much of the work of health needs assessment does not need to be duplicated by every purchasing organization. For instance, as indicated earlier, surveys of health needs in one place may carry over in an order of magnitude manner to other places; these estimates can be fine-tuned using local knowledge about the modifiers. Background work on the characteristics of various needs categories and options to meet them does not need frequent replication. Health technology assessment, futurology and so on can be centralized nationally or regionally (as in the USA).

The work involved in health needs assessment does not have to be kept 'in-house'. In fact it is important that purchasing organizations develop into outward-looking, catalysing organizations rather than remaining inward-looking bureaucracies. Other local agencies may share the health agenda and may therefore be able to carry out some of the work involved in the assessment of health need. These agencies may include the local authority departments, the probation service, voluntary sector organizations and the local research and teaching communities. They may include local people themselves. Much of the time of health needs assessment professionals within the purchasing organizations could usefully be spent fostering links and encouraging other people to share the agenda and work.

Although in some respects providers must be kept at arm's length from purchasers in order to develop strategic thinking, in other respects close collaboration is mutually beneficial. Providers have considerable resources committed in plant and staff and these cannot be altered suddenly. Thus, if significant changes to service configuration are contemplated, provider managers should be brought into the discussions at a very early stage. Indeed, they and their health professional staff should be able to make constructive suggestions about the shape and pace of progress. Whatever the nature of proposed service development the health professional staff in provider units are a valuable source of expertise.

Exploring the relationship between the health service processes and the desired health outcomes is important if change is to occur. This cannot be done by purchasers alone. Ensuring that the purchasers focus on health and quality outcomes encourages providers to explore their own practices and allows room for innovation and creativity. If purchasers concentrate on specifying processes too closely then the relationship can stultify and the problem of NHS inertia will continue. This means that both provider managers and clinicians will have an enhanced planning role. Without this enhanced role the reforms may falter as purchasers get sucked into crisis operational issues and find no time for their strategic role.

GP FUNDHOLDERS AND DISTRICT HEALTH AUTHORITY PURCHASERS

District health authorities are not the only purchasers of health care services. The NHS and Community Care Act also allowed GPs with practice lists above a certain size to contract directly with provider units for specified secondary care procedures for individual patients.

On the face of it this may seem like two completely opposing systems trying to coexist. On the one hand districts are trying to create a strategic, needs based, district-wide approach to purchasing, whereas GP fundholding encourages a demand based, individual-oriented system. Having the two approaches side by side is likely to lead to tension, but this very tension may be creative and prevent the new NHS slipping back into its bureaucratic inertia. The presence of DHA purchasers can encourage GP fundholders (and other GPs) to look more widely and proactively at the health needs of the population they wish to serve. The life cycle framework can be used by all GPs and their primary care teams to help them structure their health needs assessment process at practice or locality level.

At the same time GP fundholders can remind DHA purchasers that they need to address the needs of individuals now as well as those of the whole population at some time in the future.

COLLABORATION WITH SOCIAL SERVICES

The same tension is likely to exist between district health authority and social service purchasers. The community care part of the NHS and Community Care Act creates a purchaser–provider split within social services with the purchaser arm assessing the health and social needs of individuals who come to their attention. Again there is a need to reconcile the individual and population perspectives. This can be achieved by agreeing a joint strategic direction within which individuals' needs can be assessed.

The individual needs assessments can be very useful to the wider population based needs assessment process but it must be remembered that a population needs assessment is more than the sum of individual needs assessments. This is because the former must take into account future needs and also the needs for prevention and health promotion. The latter of course will only be carried out on those who come to the attention of social services and may exclude groups who are also in need but who for whatever reason are not referred.

Thus purchasing is a complex process, the components of which are difficult and time-consuming. If we can wrestle ourselves from the operational issues and develop a strategic, needs led role we have an unprecedented opportunity to design a health service that can truly influence the health of the people of the UK. However, purchasers alone cannot solve all the problems of the NHS. Many of the seemingly intractable problems we have been facing in the past decade, such as long waiting times, unplanned ward closures, unrestrained technological developments and the increasing inability to support care in the community, will require the commitment of both purchasers and providers of services as well as the national government and the people of the UK.

REFERENCES

1 St Leger, A. S., Schnieden, H. and Walsworth-Bell, J. P. (1992) *Evaluating Health Services' Effectiveness*. Buckingham: Open University Press.
2 Secretary of State for Health (1991) *The Health of the Nation*, Cmd 1523. London: HMSO.
3 Unwin, N. and Mercer, A. (1991) Health Needs Assessment: A pilot study in Manchester. Central, North and South Manchester Health Authorities and the Manchester Family Health Services Authority.
4 St Leger, A. S., Allen, D. and Rowsell, K. V. (1989) Procedures for evaluating innovatory proposals. *British Medical Journal*, **299**, 1017–18.

APPENDIX 1
ISSUES TO CONSIDER
WHEN SELECTING POTENTIAL
AREAS OF NEED FOR MORE
DETAILED SCRUTINY

The questions below are intended to aid a decision as to whether or not to deploy health needs assessment resources for the exploration of a possible area of unmet need. It is not suggested that the answers to all of them will be complete or wholly accurate.

1 THE SOURCE AND BACKGROUND OF THE IDEA

(a) Did the idea arise from an individual, group or organization known to have a deep interest, understanding or expertise in the suggested area of investigation?

(b) Is this a high profile or 'political' matter for which it would be expedient to be seen to do something even though there might be no other reasonable grounds for giving the matter priority?

(c) Would those proposing this investigation (assuming them to be outside the purchasing organizations) be willing to collaborate in and perhaps to contribute resources to the investigation? If so, would this provide a vehicle for strengthening relationships with the proposers for use in future work even though the suggested area of investigation might have little intrinsic merit?

2   SOURCES OF INFORMATION

(a) Is this to be an extension of the investigation of an already well documented area of need?
(b) Do there exist routinely available data or findings of studies conducted elsewhere that can throw light on the issue? If not, could a pilot study help to elucidate the potential importance of this issue?

3   WHAT IS KNOWN ABOUT THE PUTATIVE NEED

(a) Which section(s) (e.g. age group, gender, geographical location, ethnic group) of the population is likely to have this need?
(b) Is this a need related to the prevention or management of specific diseases?
(c) Is this a need related to the prevention or management of specific disabilities?
(d) Is this a need related to a person's ability to access and use already existing services?
(e) Is this a need of carers of others rather than of the ill or disabled persons themselves?
(f) Is this a population need rather than a need of identifiable individuals (e.g. in the broad sense a public health issue, such as might be tackled by altering the environment)?

4   SIZE AND IMPORTANCE OF THE PROBLEM

(a) Is there any initial indication of the number of persons who might express this need as a demand should a service be developed (or expanded)?
(b) Is it possible to quantify the severity of the need and the distribution of severity of need among the potential recipients of any service that might be developed (or expanded)?
(c) Even if quantification is not feasible is it possible to rank this need against others under consideration or likely to be under consideration?
(d) Is there evidence that the public at large view this as an important problem?
(e) Is there evidence that the groups that might have (or express) these needs regard them as an important problem?
(f) How might the groups having (or expressing) these needs rank them against any other unmet needs they have?
(g) Have the potential group of beneficiaries of the proposed needs analysis had a 'fair deal' from health and related services in the past?

5   POSSIBLE SOLUTIONS

(a) Without having studied the problems in detail is it nevertheless possible to outline the kinds of approach that would meet these needs?
(b) Would these approaches entail expansion of existing services?
(c) Would these approaches entail setting up new services and is the general nature of these services clear?

(d) Is there any evidence that the kinds of services that might emerge would be beneficial?

(e) What, in broad terms, would be the absolute costs of these services?

(f) How do these costs rank among costs of existing services?

(g) How might these services rank with others with respect to cost–benefit?

(h) Might creating new services or modifying old services lead to overall savings or increases of efficiency?

6 OPPORTUNITY COST

(a) If this area of potential need is to be explored in detail what other explorations will have to be shelved?

(b) If services to meet these putative needs are suggested then with what other resource uses will they be competing?

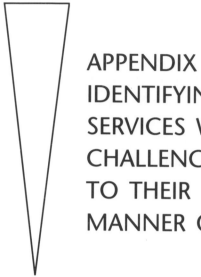

APPENDIX 2
IDENTIFYING EXISTING
SERVICES WORTHY OF
CHALLENGE WITH RESPECT
TO THEIR EXISTENCE OR
MANNER OF PROVISION

The following considerations might help to inform a decision on whether or not to allocate resources to scrutinize and, perhaps, subsequently to challenge the worth of an existing service. (The items need refining according to the context of their use, e.g. the definition of a large share in item 1.)

REASONS FOR CHALLENGING

1 A large share of resources devoted to the service.
2 The cost per patient or client is high.
3 The cost per quality-adjusted life year is high.
4 Poor comparative performance (e.g. from NHS Performance Indicators).
5 Low public perception of importance (e.g. low on Oregon style rating[1]).
6 Uncertain benefit (e.g. homeopathy and certain chemotherapy regimens).
7 Little likelihood of political flak (definitely not homeopathy, it has Royal patronage).

REASONS FOR BEING WARY OF CHALLENGING

1 Service too well established (e.g. coronary care).
2 Service high in public esteem (e.g. intensive neonatal care) – wait and see

whether public perceptions will change if the notion of opportunity cost can be put across.

3 Service backed by powerful interest groups – pick these off after the softer targets have been dealt with.

4 Service is only a placebo but is cheaper than the other services to which displaced patients or clients might subsequently be directed (e.g. homeopathy?).

REFERENCE

1 Oregon Health Service Commission (1991) *The 1991 Prioritization of Health*. Salem, OR: Oregon Health Service Commission.

APPENDIX 3
SOME ROUTINE SOURCES
OF DATA

Areas of interest	Source
Demographic data	
Estimated present population	OPCS population estimates
Five-year population projection	OPCS population projections by age bands
Ethnic information	Census, Labour Force Survey
Deprivation, Jarman 8	*British Medical Journal*, **289**, 1587–92 (1984)
Housing	National Dwelling Survey
Activity data	
Process data, hospital	Körner data, KO forms, RHAs in England (KARs), KES data
Process data, community	Körner data, KC, KT forms, RHAs in England
Hospitalization rates	Department of Health PIs, the regions
Performance indicators	Department of Health
Health and disease data	
Data relating to births	OPCS Monitor VS1
Perinatal mortality rates	OPCS Monitor VS1
Infant mortality rates	OPCS Monitor VS1

Abortions	OPCS Monitor AB
Deaths by selected causes	OPCS Monitor VS3
SMR selected causes of death	Regions
Infectious diseases	OPCS Monitors MB, WR
Morbidity	General Household Survey, Royal College of General Practitioners

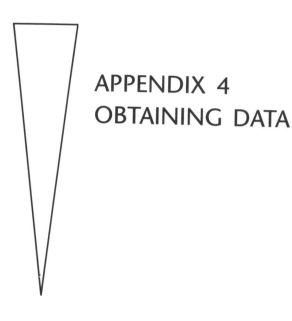

APPENDIX 4
OBTAINING DATA

INTRODUCTION

This appendix is divided into four main sections, as follows: demographic data; activity data; health and disease data; and miscellaneous information resources. The material is structured by taking subjects on which data are required and then listing the sources (see Appendix 3) where the data can be found, rather than by taking sources of data and listing what data are available from each source. This is rather clumsy when dealing with large sources of data, such as the census, but overall it facilitates finding data on a given subject.

DEMOGRAPHIC DATA

Population data

The baseline population data, from which all other population data are derived, are the results of the decennial census. The district population and the age breakdown are contained in an OPCS book called *Census 1981 – Key Statistics for Local Authorities*. 1991 census details are at the time of writing becoming available from OPCS.

The *Longitudinal Study User Manual* is obtainable from SSRU, City University, Northampton Square, London EC1V OHB.

Population estimates and projections

Population estimates refer to educated guesses of the population from the time of the last census to the present day, while population projections refer to educated guesses of the population in the future. Population estimates are calculated by OPCS by taking the census data as a baseline, by using data on births and deaths since the time of the census and then estimating migration in and out of the district. The address for OPCS is Tichfield, Fareham, Hants PO15 5RR.

Births

The Director of Public Health should be notified of all births in the district within 36 hours. Fertility rates and total births are available by legitimacy, birthweight and social class from OPCS.

Social characteristics

Most of the information available on the social characteristics of the people comes from the census. The book *Census 1981 – Key Statistics for Local Authorities*, which has already been referred to, contains the following information for districts. Similar details will be available from the 1991 Census.

- economic activity;
- industry of employment (10 per cent sample);
- travel to work (10 per cent sample);
- number of households/household size/economically active adults;
- households with children/one-adult households with children.

Note that country of birth is available from previous censuses but was not recorded in 1991. However, respondents were asked to record their self-perceived ethnic group. Thus, this book contains most of the data on social indicators that are available from the census.

As regards electoral ward data, the following information may be obtained from a regional health authority or from a local authority (all data are percentages):

- population of at least 65 years of age;
- elderly people living alone;
- population under five years of age;
- families that are one-parent families;
- workforce who are unskilled;
- workforce who are unemployed;
- households that lack basic amenities;
- population who were born in countries other than the UK.

ACTIVITY DATA

Hospital information (including day cases and outpatients)

The information systems that are at present in operation collecting hospital information are (a) Hospital Management Information System (HMIS: Körner Aggregated Returns) and (b) performance indicators.

Hospital Activity Analysis (HAA) became Körner Episode Statistics (KES) in April 1987 and included some information on psychiatric and maternity patients. HAA was introduced in 1969 by the Department of Health and Social Security (DHSS) and was a summary of the casenotes of all patients discharged from non-mental hospitals. The information was collected by medical records departments and collated regionally.

HAA was a computerized system for recording all inpatient and day case activity other than maternity and psychiatry. The coding form illustrates the large variety of information available from the system, e.g. main and other diagnoses, main and other operations, area of residence, age, sex, consultant, source of admission, disposal and length of time on the waiting list. A 10 per cent sample of information was submitted by regional health authorities to the OPCS. This formed the basis of the Hospital Inpatient Enquiry (HIPE) tables published annually. HIPE ceased at the end of 1986.

Information could be obtained from HAA on length of stay, age on admission, disposal on discharge, source of admission and cases admitted from the waiting list. In addition, there was information on diagnosis (coded according to the International Classification of Diseases), type of operation and total length of hospital stay. An HAA system for maternity was available. Information for the remaining specialty excluded from the HAA system (namely psychiatry) was recorded on the Mental Health Enquiry System (see below).

The Hospital Management Information System (HMIS), now called the Körner Aggregated Returns System (KARS) is an administrative system. It records activity but does not record either diagnoses or procedures carried out. VS forms are derived from this system. KARS data are usually recorded more completely than HAA data, and are usually processed by regional health authorities.

The Mental Health Enquiry (MHE) system recorded information about the psychiatric patients discharged from hospital. The data were sent to the DHSS at Fleetwood, where they were transferred to a computer. The MHE ceased in 1986; it was replaced from April 1987 by a system similar to HAA.

Performance indicators: the term 'performance indicator' can mean many things, but the performance indicators that are routinely available are mainly concerned with activity rather than with outcome, and so are of limited use as an epidemiological tool. There are two packages of performance indicators available, produced by (a) the DoH, and (b) the Health Services Management Centre in Birmingham. The disks run on the BBC microcomputer and also on IBM compatible machines. Information on DoH Performance Indicators can be obtained from the DoH; contact DoH, Room 1418, Euston Tower, 286 Euston Road, London NW1 3DN.

No diagnostic information is routinely recorded on day hospital patients or outpatients.

Health service activity in the community

General practitioners

Until recently little routine information was available on the activity of general practitioners. However, in the future GP annual reports to the FHSA should be a valuable source of information. At present, the FHSA should know the total number of prescriptions written by all GPs and, for one month of the year, the number of prescriptions written by each GP.

Services to the community

These include:

- vaccination and immunization, obtainable from Körner statistics;
- family planning services, obtainable from Körner statistics;
- school health services, obtainable from form 8MI;
- maternity and child health services, obtainable from Körner statistics.

HEALTH AND DISEASE DATA

This section is divided into four parts as follows: mortality data, morbidity data, health status and health outcome.

Mortality data

A copy of the death registration of every resident who dies in the district or elsewhere is sent to the Director of Public Health Medicine. District mortality data are processed by OPCS and are available as VS returns. They contain some details of the number of people who died in the district from a large number of conditions (using the ICD code). The data are presented by age and sex.

The OPCS provides 'death tapes' to regions. Before 1981 data did not include ward and postcode, but subsequently they have been included. It is now possible to build up a map of deaths by ward for a district from these tapes. Analysis can be aided by using a computer program to interrogate the database. *FIND* is a computer program developed by Dr Whitten of the School of Environmental Science at the University of Bradford for this purpose. The selection criteria include: particulars of registration, sex, cause of death, particulars of occupation, place of birth, date of birth, date of death, postcode and ward.

Morbidity data

Infectious diseases

Episodes of notifiable infectious diseases are reported to the local authority Proper Officer, who is usually a consultant in public health medicine. The Communicable Disease Surveillance Centre (CDSC) produces the *Communicable Disease Report* (*CDR*) weekly. The *CDR* lists the number of cases of the more common infectious diseases, which have been diagnosed in the public health laboratories around the country. It also contains reports on interesting outbreaks and cases of infectious diseases.

Prescribable disease

Data on the number of prescribable (occupational certifiable) diseases are available from the Health and Safety Executive.

Neoplastic diseases

Incidence data on patients with malignant neoplasms (and a few benign neoplasms) are compiled by the Cancer Registry.

Incidence of diseases in the community

There is no routine system of measuring disease incidence in the community. Körner collects information on the diagnoses of people who are admitted to hospital, but in most conditions the number of hospital admissions for a condition is a poor measure of its incidence in the community, partly because not everyone with a given disease will be treated in hospital, and partly because Körner reflects events rather than patients.

Health status

Ideally information should be available on the health status of your district. To obtain this, a local survey is usually necessary. An example is the health survey of Stockport Health Authority residents, which was based on a random sample of 1 per cent of Stockport residents.

Health outcome

This can be measured in a number of ways; for example, the mortality or morbidity resulting from a procedure, or the effect of a procedure on the quality of life. From the district point of view, mortality data are the easiest to obtain; death certificates of every resident who dies in the district, or elsewhere, are sent to the Director of Public Health. Morbidity is more difficult, and a local survey may be necessary. The Royal College of General Practitioners has published data on morbidity in general practice.[1,2] The Nottingham Health Profile and many other instruments have been used to assess improvements in the quality of life following procedures.[3]

MISCELLANEOUS INFORMATION RESOURCES

Contract Minimum Data Set (CMDS)

The CMDS was introduced to meet the exigencies of contracting. It is essentially KES with the addition of patient names and addresses and a contract identifier to each patient episode. Purchasers have access, via the contract identifiers, to the records of their own residents. At the time of writing there is no nationally agreed policy with regard to purchasers having access to additional information. It seems likely that CMDS will subsume KES.

Developing Information Systems for Purchasers (DISP)

DISP has arisen from a Department of Health initiative to support the specific information requirements of purchasers. It is envisaged to have six interrelated modules:

- contract management;
- invoice processing;
- population health register;
- health event linkage;
- health needs assessment and planning;
- management information system.

Four flagship sites have been funded to develop and pilot parts of the system. However, RHAs are free to develop their own versions.

The population health register will probably be based on or linked to the FHSA age–sex registers. Health event linkage might entail maintaining longitudinal records of each individual's contact with primary, secondary and, possibly, social services, and also recording events such as cancer registrations and deaths. Whether this potentially exciting module will come into being will depend upon the solving of technical matters of data capture and linkage, and the resolution of issues of privacy and confidentiality. The health needs assessment module is likely to be a set of software tools to aid the electronic gathering of routinely available data on health from diverse sources, analysis of those data and presentation of the findings for use in needs assessment. The management information system will provide a similar set of tools to aid managers in other tasks connected with purchasing.

Public health common data set for England and Wales

The public health common data set is sponsored by the Department of Health and compiled by the Institute of Public Health of the University of Surrey (Guildford, Surrey GU2 5XH) from data supplied by the OPCS. Thus for each calendar year (since the late 1980s) it draws together in a convenient form much of the OPCS data mentioned elsewhere in our life cycle chapters and these appendices.

The data set contains statistics pertaining to each DHA resident population in England and Wales and aggregate RHA and national figures. The information comes under three headings: demography, fertility and mortality. The demographic section contains population estimates, population projections, an underprivileged area score and information about ethnic composition. The section on fertility contains a variety of statistics, which include information about fertility rates, live births by maternal age, percentage of low birth-weight babies, stillbirths and abortions. The section on mortality contains death rates and SMRs for selected causes of infant, child and adult death. It highlights deaths from 'avoidable' and other potentially reducible causes of death. There are some statistics on population years of life lost attributable to selected causes of death.

The common data set is distributed to all regional and district departments of public health medicine. It comes on IBM compatible microcomputer floppy disks in a format readable by the spreadsheet program *Lotus 1-2-3*. The Lotus 1-2-3 spreadsheet file format has become almost an industry standard and hence there are many proprietary spreadsheet packages that can access the common data set. Periodically information contained in the data set and analyses based on it are published in printed form by the DoH.

REFERENCES

1 Royal College of General Practitioners (1986) *Morbidity Statistics from General Practice: Third National Study*. London: HMSO.
2 Royal College of General Practitioners (1990) *Morbidity Statistics from General Practice: Third National Study, Socio-economic Analyses*. London: HMSO.
3 Wilkin, D., Hallam, L. and Daggett, M. (1992) *Measures of Need and Outcome for Primary Health Care*. Oxford: Oxford University Press.

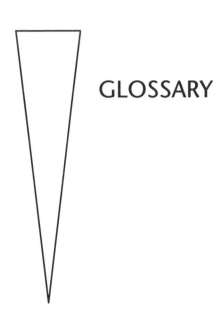

GLOSSARY

The glossary contains terms found in this book and in related works to which the reader might refer. It is intended to be particularly helpful to readers with little prior medical knowledge or experience of the health service.

acute disease: disease of short duration.

age effect: the health experience of a birth cohort is partly determined by the age of its members.

agoraphobia: a disordered fear of open places; this creates severe anxiety on leaving the home.

amphetamine: a stimulant drug often misused to induce euphoria; can be taken by mouth, snorted or injected.

anthropological: to do with anthropology; anthropology is the study of the behaviour of human groups and populations.

arithmetic mean: the sum of a series of like measurements divided by the number of items summed; a variety of 'average'.

association: is present when one variable alters in a consistent manner as another changes; association is necessary for causation but does not establish causation.

average: 'typical' value of a measurement taken on all members of a sample or population; assumed to be the arithmetic mean unless otherwise stated.

benzodiazepine drugs: a group of medicines which act as either day-time tranquillizers, e.g. Valium, or as sleeping tablets e.g. Mogadon.

bias: the tendency for measurements to depart systematically from their true values.

biometry: the study of the measurable properties of biological material, including humans; a branch of applied statistics.

birth cohort: a group of people born at or around the same time.

carcinogen: something (e.g. a chemical) known to cause cancer.

cardiovascular disease: any disease of the heart or main blood vessels.

causality (criteria for): (a) theoretical plausibility; (b) the assumed cause is shown to precede the effect; (c) strength of association; (d) dose–response relationship; (e) specificity of effect by presumed cause; (f) coherence of circumstantial evidence of diverse kinds; (g) direct experimental evidence.

causal relationship: changes in one variable (the effect) are *brought about* by changes in another (the cause) and are not merely findings incidental on *both* variables being the effect of a deeper cause. Causality is a philosophical notion not strictly provable in the real world; however, we act on the assumption that it pertains.

census: official numbering of population and gathering of other statistics (e.g. type of housing).

cerebro-vascular disease: disease where the brain is affected by problems with the blood vessels; this often results in strokes.

chance events: events that are unpredictable in the present state of knowledge; see *probability.*

chronic disease: disease of long duration; also, a confusing usage in the term chronic disease epidemiology, meaning the study of non-communicable disease.

circulatory disease: another term for cardiovascular disease.

cohort: a group of people defined by a common characteristic and followed up over time; see also *birth cohort.*

cohort effect: the influence on the health of a *birth cohort* consequential upon the era in which they were born.

confidence interval: range of values within which a quantity estimated from a series of observations is believed to lie. The calculation takes account of the variation inherent to the data and the statistical distribution (e.g. Gaussian) the data are assumed to follow. The degree of confidence that the true value lies within the interval is expressed as the probability that the interval, or any similar one calculated from a (hypothetical) series of replications of the study, contains the value of the quantity being estimated.

confidence limits: the values bounding a *confidence interval.*

congenital: present from birth.

coronary heart disease: also known as ischaemic heart disease. The coronary arteries are blood vessels that provide oxygen to the heart muscle; if they become narrowed or blocked a person is said to be suffering from ischaemic or coronary heart disease. The heart muscle being short of oxygen can lead to pain (angina), a disordered rhythm of the heart or death of part of the heart muscle; this is known as a 'heart attack' or acute myocardial infarction (MI).

correlation: the degree to which two variables associate. If each pair of values of the variables is plotted on a graph then there is said to be correlation if the scatter of points is non-random. Commonly used measures of linear correlation (e.g. product moment and Spearman) are portrayed as a number whose magnitude varies according the closeness of the scatter of points to some straight line. A value near zero will arise if there is little or no correlation (random scatter). A value of +1 means that the points lie exactly on a straight line passing upwards from left to right on the graph. A value of –1 means that the points lie exactly on a straight line passing downwards from left to right. However, beware of pitfalls; see *spurious correlation*.

cost–benefit: economic analysis whereby all costs and benefits associated with a service are translated into the same units (usually financial) and related to one another (e.g. cost/benefit ratio) to facilitate comparison of different service options.

cost-effectiveness: economic analysis by which different means of achieving the same outcome are compared in terms of costs.

cost–utility: a class of economic techniques that relate cost to some measure of utility (or usefulness) of outcome; the best known examples are *cost–benefit* and *cost per QALY* analysis.

cost per QALY: cost per quality adjusted life year; see *quality adjusted life year*.

crude rate: the total number of events (e.g. deaths) arising from a defined population during a specified time and divided by the size of the relevant population; no attempt is made to adjust the rate to facilitate comparison with populations having a different structure (e.g. age composition); see *standardized mortality ratio*.

data: the measurements (recordings etc.) assembled during a study.

death rate: number of deaths arising from a specified population during the course of one year represented as a proportion of the number at risk of dying (the population); death rates can be age-, cause- and gender-specific; they can be used to estimate the probability of death.

denominator: the bottom line in the division of two numbers to form a ratio, proportion or rate.

DHA: see *district health authority*.

digestive disease: a collective term for diseases of the organs of digestion from the mouth through the small bowel to the large bowel, rectum and anus.

district health authority (DHA): the lowest tier of statutory body in England responsible for the health care of geographically defined populations; Scotland, Wales and Northern Ireland have similar arrangements but use different names.

dose–response relationship: the finding that as the magnitude of a putative causal agent changes so also does the magnitude of its putative effect (response of the system under study) and that this occurs in a consistent manner; usually as dose increases so does response, but eventually the increases in response become ever-smaller.

edentulous: having no teeth.

effectiveness: a measure of the degree to which a service provides benefit to a community.

efficacy: a measure of the degree to which a treatment, procedure or caring regimen provides benefit to the individual.

efficiency: the relationship between input and output of health care in cost terms; an efficient service is one that maximizes output for a given input, or minimizes input for a fixed output.

endocrine: pertaining to the endocrine system (glands), which produces hormones. Hormones are chemical regulators of bodily functions.

epidemiology: study of the distribution and determinants of disease in populations.

evaluation of health services' effectiveness: the critical assessment, on as objective a basis as possible, of the degree to which entire services or their component parts (e.g. diagnostic tests, treatments and caring procedures) fulfil stated goals.

family health services authority: statutory bodies responsible for planning and administering primary care services for geographically defined populations (these populations are often, but not always, coterminous with DHA populations).

fixed costs: the basic costs that have to be met before there can be any production, e.g. a hospital ward requires equipment and staff.

health education: educating the public to promote and maintain their health.

health index: a composite of several *health indicators.*

health indicator: a measure of health status or of some (proxy) factor associated with health status.

health promotion: the formulation and promotion of legislation, policies, educational services and specific services to enable individual members of the community to maximize their potential for a healthy life.

health status index: a summary measure of the overall health experience of a defined population; such indices may encompass physical function, ability to cope with daily living, mental well-being, etc.

hospice: a centre providing care for terminally ill people and support for their relatives.

hydrocephalus: excess fluid within the cavities of the brain leading to damage of brain tissue; it is often associated with spina bifida.

incidence rate: the number of new cases of a disease arising in a defined population during a specified period of time; the rate is formed from the ratio of the number of new cases to the size of the population from which they arose.

incident cases: new cases of disease arising during a specified period of time.

index: a descriptive measure or marker.

indicator: a proxy or pseudo-measurement giving an 'indication' of what a more precise and/or valid measuring instrument might show, e.g. mortality statistics are used as indicators of morbidity.

inguinal hernia: a weak spot in the abdominal wall leading to protrusion of abdominal contents; also known as a 'rupture'.

International Classification of Disease (ICD): a classification of disease promulgated by the World Health Organization and used routinely within health services and in epidemiological research.

ischaemic heart disease: see *coronary heart disease.*

Jarman score: a score of social deprivation derived from census data. It uses eight variables weighted according to how much they are thought to increase the workload of GPs. The eight variables are: old people living alone; children aged under five; single-parent households; unskilled people; unemployed people; overcrowded households; people who have moved house; ethnic minority households.

Körner Episode System: a system of data collection in the National Health Service.

It counts the number of episodes of admission to hospital for each speciality and consultant; it collects data on diagnoses, place of residence and whether the admission ended in death or discharge.

life tables: (a) Current: tabular representation of the mortality experience of a population, the members of which are at different ages, at a point in time; from this may be calculated summary statistics, such as expectation of life at birth, of the population's current mortality. (b) Cohort: as current but portraying the actual mortality experience of a birth cohort of individuals who have been followed over time; true expectations of life can be calculated for (nearly) extinct cohorts, e.g. persons born in 1890.

lymphoma: cancer of the lymph glands.

MacMillan nurses: nurses specially trained to work with people suffering from cancer and with their families; they often work within the health service but are employed by the MacMillan Trust, an independent voluntary organization.

mammographic breast screening: a technique by which an X-ray (mammogram) of the breast is taken on women who have no symptoms of disease in order to reveal changes to the breast tissue indicative of early (and supposedly 'curable') cancer; in the UK screening is offered routinely every five years to women aged between 50 and 70 years.

marginal cost: the cost of extra items of production (e.g. each extra patient treated) on the assumption that fixed costs will not have to increase.

mean: see *arithmetic mean.*

MENCAP: a voluntary society, which promotes the welfare of the mentally handicapped.

metabolic disease: a disease caused by a disturbance of the metabolism; metabolism is the process by which the body converts food into energy and growth, removes waste, maintains itself, etc.

MIND: a voluntary society, which promotes the welfare of the mentally ill.

monitoring: continuing measurement of a variety of indicators of health care need, health service process, or health outcomes to identify potential problems; cf surveillance.

monopoly: situation in which there is a sole supplier of goods or services, with a consequent ability to maintain price without restraint of competition.

monopsony: situation in which there is a sole purchaser of goods or services, with a consequent ability to force price down.

morbidity: ill-health.

musculo-skeletal: pertaining to muscles, bones and joints.

need: persons with health-related need may, for the purposes of health care planning, pragmatically be defined thus: as those for whom some policy, preventive service, treatment or caring regimen, provided by any agency but of proven worth, can offer benefit.

neonatology: the medical specialty concerned with the treatment of new-born babies.

neoplasm: a new (abnormal) growth; malignant neoplasm is another way of saying cancer.

NHS and Community Care Act 1990: an Act of the British Parliament bringing about radical change to the structure of the National Health Service.

numerator: the top line of the division of one number by another to form a ratio, proportion or rate.

obstetric: pertaining to the process of birth.

occupational social class: classification of the population using the occupation of the head of household; it is used as an indicator of socio-economic status. It is summarized thus:

I	(e.g. major professions and senior management)
II	(e.g. lesser professions and middle management)
III non-manual	(skilled 'white collar' workers)
III manual	(skilled manual workers)
IV	(semi-skilled workers)
V	(unskilled workers)
VI	(not otherwise classifiable).

The classification of occupations is extremely complicated and requires guidance from a detailed rubric prepared by the Registrar General.

oesophagus: the gullet, the tube connecting the mouth and the stomach.

oncology: the medical specialty concerned with the treatment of cancer.

opportunity cost: the lost opportunity, once money is spent, to spend it on something else.

osteoporosis: thinning of the bones.

outlier: an observation of a magnitude that is extremely unusual in the context of the variation exhibited by the generality of the data; this may be a measurement or recording error, or an exciting observation needing explanation.

parasuicide: deliberate self-injury (e.g. by taking a drug inappropriately), which has the appearance of an attempted suicide but in which suicidal intent cannot definitely be inferred.

period effect: an influence on the health of a birth cohort attributable to events (e.g. an influenza outbreak) at some period in calendar time; different birth cohorts will be at different stages in their life cycles when exposed to the event and thus may be affected differently.

preconceptual: before conception.

presymptomatic: the stage of a disease before symptoms develop.

prevalence ratio: the number of existing cases of a disease in a defined population as a ratio of the size of that population; if this is defined for a point in time then a point prevalence ratio is obtained; if it is defined for a specified time period then a period prevalence ratio is obtained.

prevalent cases: the number of cases of existing disease at a specified point in time.

probability: chance of an event occurring; represented as a number between zero (event cannot occur) and one (must occur); sometimes expressed as a percentage.

prognosis: the statistical distribution(s) of outcomes from a population of patients with a common diagnosis; treatment, if successful, beneficially alters these distributions.

proportion: a ratio in which an integer (whole number) numerator, e.g. cases, is a subset of an integer denominator, e.g. the population; proportions range between zero and one.

provider: an organization (e.g. a hospital) which sells services to *purchasers* of health care.

proxy measure: a measure or indicator of some specific attribute which because that attribute is closely related to a second attribute serves as an indirect measure of the second attribute; e.g. mortality rates are proxy measures of morbidity.

psychogeriatrics: the medical specialty concerned with the mental health of the elderly.

public health medicine: the medical speciality concerned with the study and promotion of health in populations and communities.

purchaser: a body (e.g. a district health authority or fund-holding general practitioner) that assesses the health needs of a defined population and buys services to meet those needs from *providers* (e.g. hospitals).

quality adjusted life year (QALY): a number of years of life with ill-health (or disability) scaled to an equivalent, lesser, number of years with perfect health (or freedom from disability).

rate: a proportion for which the numerator accumulates (or is collected) over a defined period of time.

ratio: one number divided by another.

respiratory disease: a collective term for diseases of the organs used in breathing.

risk factor: a factor known to be associated with an increased incidence of a disease; this association may be purely statistical and not proven to represent a causal influence of the factor on the disease.

salpingitis: inflammation of the fallopian tubes.

sample: subset of a population chosen for study in the expectation that information yielded by the sample will convey information about the population.

sampling frame: list (ideally) containing each individual of the population from which it is planned to draw a sample for detailed scrutiny.

sickle cell anaemia: a congenital disorder of the blood occurring predominantly in people of Afro-Caribbean or African origin.

significance test: a statistical procedure for aiding decisions about whether the observed difference of an estimated quantity (e.g. a mean or a difference between means) from a set value is due to chance fluctuation consequent upon the particular sample selected or represents a genuine characteristic of the population(s) from which the sample(s) was taken.

simple random sample: sample selected in a manner such that it and all other possible samples of the same size taken from the sampling frame have an equal chance of being chosen.

social class: see *occupational social class.*

spina bifida: a congenital malformation of the spinal cord, usually causing paralysis of the lower limbs; sometimes it is associated with hydrocephalus.

spurious correlation: (a) Arises when the change in a variable is plotted against the initial value, e.g. reduction in blood pressure following treatment versus level of blood pressure before treatment. (b) Arises when there is an *outlying* pair of observations far from the main cluster of essentially uncorrelated pairs of observations. (c) misleading lack of (linear) correlation, i.e. correlation coefficient near zero; arises when the measurements are associated but the form of association is very non-linear (e.g. a U shaped curve).

standardized mortality ratio (SMR): the number of deaths arising in a population expressed as a ratio to the number expected in that time period if members of the population had at each age the same risk of dying as those of a standard (or reference) population.

statistic: a measure calculated from data; this may be an estimate of a parameter of a statistical model or frequency distribution (e.g. an average), or the index of a significance test (e.g. the chi squared statistic).

surveillance: systematic and regular collection and analysis of indicators of health, health need, health service process and health service outcome in order to facilitate rapid identification of potential problems, initiation of detailed investigation, and implementation of control measures; cf *monitoring.*

systematic sample: sample selected by working systematically through a sampling frame, e.g. selecting every tenth member.

teratogen: a factor known to increase the risk of fetal malformation.

theory: an attempt to understand and explain the behaviour of some aspect of the world of our experience. A theory is *scientific* if it is capable of making predictions that are testable and that if falsified would cause doubt about the utility of the theory. Informal properties of a good theory are simplicity (elegance), plausibility, explanatory power and a capacity to be 'visualized' or to stimulate creative imagination.

Townsend score: a measure of social deprivation using four variables from census data. These variables are: unemployed people; households with no car; households not owner occupied; overcrowded households. These produce a 'Z score'. The average electoral ward in the area scores 0. Any ward with a negative score is, supposedly, more deprived than the average and any score above 0 is, supposedly, less deprived than the average.

validated measure: a measure that has been subjected to *validation.*

validation: procedures whereby measuring instruments are demonstrated to produce measurements with properties consistent with expectations derived from the theoretical perspective that led to that kind of measurement being sought, i.e. whether the instrument measures what it purports to measure.

FURTHER READING

Abramson, J. H. (1986) *Survey Methods in Community Medicine: An Introduction to Epidemiological and Evaluative Studies*. London: Churchill Livingstone.

Armitage, P. and Berry, G. (1987) *Statistical Methods in Medical Research*. Oxford: Blackwell.

Armstrong, D. (1989) *An Outline of Sociology as Applied to Medicine*. Bristol: Wright.

Ashton, J. (ed.) (1991) *Healthy Cities*. Milton Keynes: Open University Press.

Ashton, J. and Seymour, H. (1988) *The New Public Health*. Milton Keynes: Open University Press.

Bland, M. (1988) *An Introduction to Medical Statistics*. Oxford: Oxford University Press.

Bowling, A. (1991) *Measuring Health – A Review of Quality of Life Measurement Scales*. Milton Keynes: Open University Press.

Cochrane, A. L. (1972) *Effectiveness and Efficiency: Random Reflections on Health Services*. Oxford: Nuffield Provincial Hospitals Trust.

Hennekens, C. and Buring, J. (1987) *Epidemiology in Medicine*. Boston: Little, Brown and Co.

Holland, W. W. (ed.) (1983) *Evaluation of Health Care*. Oxford: Oxford University Press.

Last, J. M. (ed.) (1988) *A Dictionary of Epidemiology*. Oxford: Oxford University Press.

McDowell, I. and Newall, C. (1987) *Measuring Health – A Guide to Rating Scales and Questionnaires*. Oxford: Oxford University Press.

McKeown, T. (1976) *The Role of Medicine – Dream, Mirage or Nemesis?* London: The Nuffield Provincial Hospitals Trust.

McNeill, P. (1990) *Research Methods.* London: Routledge.

Medawar, P. B. (1970) *Induction and Intuition in Scientific Thought.* London: Methuen.

Morgan, M., Calnan, M. and Manning, N. (1985) *Sociological Approaches to Health and Health Care.* London: Croom Helm.

Moser, C. A. and Kacton, G. (1986) *Survey Methods in Social Investigation.* Aldershot: Gower.

Oldham, P. D. (1968) *Measurement in Medicine: The Interpretation of Numerical Data.* London: English Universities Press.

Rothman, K. (1986) *Modern Epidemiology.* Boston: Little, Brown and Co.

St Leger, A. S., Schnieden, H. and Walsworth-Bell, J. P. (1992) *Evaluating Health Services' Effectiveness – A Guide for Health Professionals, Service Managers and Policy Makers.* Buckingham: Open University Press.

Sutton, C. (1987) *A Handbook of Research for the Helping Professions.* London: Routledge and Kegan Paul.

Townsend, P. and Davidson, N. (1982) *Inequalities in Health* (the Black Report). Harmondsworth: Penguin.

Walker, S. R. and Rosser, R. M. (eds) (1987) *Quality of Life Assessment and Its Applications.* Lancaster: MTP Press.

Wilkin, D., Hallam, L. and Daggett, M. (1992) *Measures of Need and Outcome for Primary Health Care.* Oxford: Oxford University Press.

Woodward, M. and Francis, L. M. (1988) *Statistics for Health Management and Research.* London: Edward Arnold (Hodder and Stoughton).

INDEX